# Praise for
# Inner Leadership

"*Inner Leadership* takes a different and remarkable approach to leadership as a journey of discovery. Anyone who wants to realize his or her leadership potential can follow a carefully described path that is rich with illustrative examples and insightful exercises.
I recommend *Inner Leadership* to anyone who is committed to transforming and empowering themselves or organizations for superior results."
Raj Dhingra, *Vice President, 3Com Corporation*

"This is a highly accessible book, with simple and powerful concepts that can be applied from the first moment you read them, which can make a significant difference to how you perceive yourself and how others perceive you."
Amanda Alexander, *Partner, KPMG*

"This book and its contents should be made available to every new employee coming into organizations. As an investment, it would lay the foundation for developing the next generation of personally aware and confident individuals, energized team members and sensitive people managers."
*Richard Knight, HR Transition Manager, Pricewaterhouse Coopers*

"A fascinating and stimulating piece of work. Smith encourages us to look at ourselves as individual leaders and examines, through a series of simple exercises and case studies, what enables us – and disables us – to achieve our goals. To realize that one's potential, in the workplace and outside, is totally unlimited, and that the word 'can't' need not exist in our inner vocabulary, is one of the many powerful conclusions."
*Rob MacMillan, Consulting Manager, Nicholson International*

This book is dedicated

to my mother and father, for their love and care;

to Jane, whose love and passion encourage me to redefine myself again and again;

and to Hannah, whose love and presence in my life have brought me joy.

# INNER LEADERSHIP

*people skills for professionals*

The business agenda at the start of the twenty-first century focuses on working with change and developing people's potential and performance.
The *People Skills for Professionals* series brings this leading theme to life with a range of practical human resource guides for anyone who wants to get the best from their people in the world of the learning organization.

## Other Titles in the Series

# INNER LEADERSHIP

## REALize Your

## Self-Leading Potential

## Simon Smith

NICHOLAS BREALEY
PUBLISHING
LONDON

First published by
Nicholas Brealey Publishing Limited in 2000

36 John Street
London
WC1N 2AT, UK
Tel: +44 (0)20 7430 0224
Fax: +44 (0)20 7404 8311

1163 E. Ogden Avenue, Suite 705-229
Naperville
IL 60563-8535, USA
Tel: (888) BREALEY
Fax: (630) 898 3595

http://www.nbrealey-books.com

http://www.Inner-Leadership.com

Illustrations by Steve Simpson

ISBN 1-85788-271-7

**Library of Congress Cataloging-in-Publication Data**

Smith, Simon (Simon James)
 Inner Leadership : REALize your self-leading potential / Simon Smith ;
illustrations by Steve Simpson.
  p.   cm.
 Includes bibliographical references and index.
 ISBN 1-85788-271-7
 1. Leadership.  2. Self-perception.  3. Management.  I. Title.
 HD57.7 .S654 2000
 650.1—dc21                                                 00-020498

**British Library Cataloguing in Publication Data**
A catalogue record for this book is available from the British Library.

Printed in Finland by Werner Söderström Oy.

# Contents

# *Preface*

I wrote this book because I know we all have enormous
unrealized potential within ourselves, which we can use to
transform and improve our organizations and our lives.
Unfortunately, it often remains unrealized. Most people
underestimate themselves, not realizing the qualities and
potential they possess. Even fewer know how to access these.
*Inner Leadership* will enable you to recognize the deep resources
you have and apply them, taking the lead wherever you are in
your organization.

   *Inner Leadership* is for you if you are willing to take the lead and
work at your own leading edge by taking the initiative, by
exceling yourself and inspiring others to do the same, whether or
not imbued with the authority to do so. Leading is often narrowly
defined as being confined to the top few people in a company.
But there are potential leaders in all parts of an organization,
representing a huge resource of creativity and enthusiasm.

   This broader definition of leadership fits many modern
companies and the people who make them successful. It is
especially prevalent in knowledge-based businesses, for
example, where if you excel yourself it is possible to make a
significant difference. Such people are often not seen as leaders.
You may work quite independently in large or small, hierarchical

or 'flat' organizations, or as independent consultants. You may work as information systems designers, IT consultants, economists, marketing strategists, accountants, lawyers, venture capitalists, research scientists, psychologists, trainers, technologists and product designers, architects and engineers, organizational development consultants or in many other roles.

You are the people whose ideas, creativity and inspiration are the lifeblood of your organizations. My aim is to help you take the lead and apply more of yourself, your qualities and your deep resources to the work situations facing you, in order to fulfill more of your and your organization's potential. The emphasis is on *you*. The most effective people are those able to respond to the real needs of new situations as they happen. The most successful companies need to be full of people who are able to do that, full of self-leaders.

Corporate transformation can only take place where there is individual transformation. As Dr W Edwards Deming said: 'Nothing changes without personal transformation.'[1] Yet personal transformation has not been within the remit of organizations. People are required to see themselves and their organizations in a wider or different context before change can take place, but scant attention has been given to how to achieve this. When a number of individuals practicing inner leadership come together, they can combine in a far more powerful, creative and effective way than ever before.

Imagine you are able to see situations crystal clearly and respond to what is really needed. Imagine you feel free to make whatever decisions and take whatever actions you believe are right. Imagine you are aware of what is happening inside you, what unconscious forces, expectations, assumptions and fears influence your view of life and stop you making the most appropriate response. Imagine you have a far greater diversity of qualities, talents and resources than you think. Imagine you have strong and clear values and a purpose that shape the way you respond and express who you want to be. Then you could realize your self-leading potential, your ability to respond to the real needs of each situation, and be creative, make clear decisions and work at your leading edge.

Stop imagining. *Inner Leadership* shows you how.

# Acknowledgments

I thank David England, my best man and business partner, for his thoughts and insights and for keeping so much going while I wrote the book.

I thank all those who read draft versions of the book and gave me valuable feedback and case studies: John Dixon, Jane Morrell, Peter Smith, John Marston, Mette Marston, Angus Landman, Georgina Weaver, Sue Arnold, Sue Valentine, Chris Bligh, Richard Knight, Rod Aspinwall, Amanda Alexander and Pat Morris.

I thank Helen Porter and Sue Coll for their wonderful editing.

I thank Nick Brealey for backing me with time, patience and resources.

I thank Steve Simpson for his deep understanding of the concepts and process of inner leadership and for the humor and skill with which he has illustrated this book.

# Inner Leadership 1

Sir Francis Drake sailed *The Golden Hind* around the world between 1577 and 1580, a great feat. It took 80 men to sail the ship. Their roles were narrowly defined within a tight, hierarchical structure. Drake's purpose was to explore new lands and find gold and other valuable treasure, but most of his crew were not beneficiaries of this purpose and would not have identified with it. They were required merely to carry out orders. Any disagreement, even in the form of ideas, would have been seen as mutiny.

In this model the captain is the traditional leader, the officers the managers and the ordinary seamen the employees. As the ship was run according to the hierarchical command-and-control model, there was little room for creativity. Everyone would pull together to save their own skins in times of crisis, but not in the normal course of events. It was a tough world where a great deal of energy was expended on forcing people to do things in a prescribed way. Over 400 years later, many organizations are still run along these lines.

## MODERN LEADERSHIP – ADAPTIVE AND AWARE

By contrast, *Team Philips* is a very modern sailing vessel, built for a round-the-world race in 2000. Just six people sail it. Its design is revolutionary, sleek and fast, made with the most technologically advanced materials. For speed, it is designed to sail as close to the wind as possible. Every crew member is totally committed to give their best. Success depends on each of them being aware and making decisions about what is happening. They are required to be multiskilled, with knowledge of the whole process of sailing the vessel. Everyone is required to achieve personal excellence, to work together and to inspire each other. They have a common vision, to win the race.

There is still a skipper, Pete Goss, but he will want to know others' opinions in order to build a broader picture of reality at any given moment. This leaves him in a more accountable and vulnerable position than a traditional leader. His performance will be understood by his colleagues for what it is. Everyone on board has a contribution to make. They are all more accountable and responsible. Every person will be working to maximum capacity for the whole voyage in order to achieve their collective purpose.

The difference is clear. *Team Philips* has not one captain but a whole crew of leaders, filled with knowledge, determination and inspiration. One person not pulling their weight – or exceling themselves – will make a difference to performance. The change in attitude between the sixteenth and twenty-first centuries makes as much difference to performance as do technological advances.

Modern organizations require people to be more exposed and more accountable. Everyone needs to think and to take risks, to suggest ideas that may be wrong and to see how they can improve things, to focus on the end goal of providing customers with services and products that deliver value. Everyone must use their knowledge, apply it and turn it into something valuable. People are required to stand by what they know and make their own judgments, even if this goes against 'the rules'.

Leaders are people willing to:

- meet the real needs of each situation with awareness, aptitude and purpose;
- operate at the edge of their abilities and their creativity;
- take responsibility and be accountable for their actions;
- expose themselves to risk and stand up for their convictions;
- see the bigger picture and apply their insight to meeting objectives;
- strive for excellence;
- improve things wherever they are in an organization;
- inspire others to give of their best;
- open themselves to challenge and seek to understand others' viewpoints;
- approach work with courage, passion, humanity, purpose and spirit.

This kind of leadership requires inner strength more than techniques and skills. It requires your spirit. It requires you to recognize and explore the many parts of yourself and bring them together in a powerful, integrated whole. It requires you to explore your basic assumptions about yourself, your life and your work. It requires you to differentiate yourself from the situation and the task in front of you. It asks you to make use of all your resources and to respond to the real needs of each situation appropriately.

I have seen many instances where people have been unable to respond to the real needs of a situation, for example:

- major mergers called off because the senior directors could not agree on roles and job titles;
- a company going bankrupt as a result of false information being given to directors, to protect the CEO's self-image;
- another company going bankrupt as a result of a

disastrous acquisition that the finance director knew was unwise, but failed to oppose;
- a promising career ended abruptly because the manager could not accept constructive criticism;
- a board of directors fighting and humiliating each other as they jostled for power, with no regard for the well-being of the company;
- unnecessary and costly misunderstandings as a result of people being unable to hear what others are really saying;
- superb creative ideas scotched because the CEO had not thought of them and good people leaving because the CEO took all the credit for their ideas.

By contrast, I have seen a hardline Glaswegian trade unionist support a buyout of his company that he had at first vociferously opposed. He was able to change his stance once he realized it was in the company's and its employees' best interests. He transformed his own principles from dogma to a response to the real needs of the people he served. He stood by this even in the face of criticism by some who saw it as a massive U-turn.

And then there's George. George always aims to respond to the needs of the situations he is given to manage. He has had seven positions in ten years. Within two years he has usually worked himself out of a job, by training others to take the lead, or by selling or outsourcing the function, doing whatever is of the greatest benefit to his organization. He works for one of the largest companies in the UK. He has a reputation for clarity, effectiveness and integrity. Now he is running one of the company's most important new projects and is close to attaining a main board position. George has learned to make decisions on the basis of courage and awareness, not out of fear for his own future.

*Everyone is a leader*

These are the people whose ideas, creativity and inspiration can make an enormous difference to a venture's success or failure. They have independent minds and they take risks, putting their own reputations on the line. They have their own ideas and their own values. If they think wrong decisions are being made, they will dissent and may even leave. If they want something to happen, they will make sure it does.

Another excellent example is the development of one of the biggest-selling drugs of all time, Losec, which was completed in secret by two scientists at Swedish pharmaceutical company Astra, despite several instructions by top management to stop the project. The scientists understood the drug's potential and they refused to give up when they encountered problems. They were prepared to put their jobs on the line to achieve their goal. They were not in positions of traditional leadership, but they were real leaders and they created huge value for that company.

> Leadership has to take place every day. It cannot be the responsibility of a few, a rare event. A leader, above or below, with or without authority, has to engage people in confronting the challenge, adjusting their values, changing perspectives and learning new habits.
> Heifetz and Laurie, *The Work of Leadership*[1]

Raj Dhingra is a vice-president running a division of 3Com that contributes a significant portion of the technology group's revenues and a higher than average profit margin. Market leader in its field, the division has been very successful. Looking ahead, Raj told me:

> If we are to stay on top in our field and lead the changes in technology and the market applications, we must end the culture of the heroic leader, where people look upwards all the time for decisions. What I want to create here is a culture where everyone is a leader, empowered and confident to make the decisions they are able to make. To do that, we need to change people's attitudes and get them thinking differently about themselves and the company. Then we can create a really successful company for the future, capable of reinventing itself.

Raj has a vision of a company full of leaders, where initiative and creativity abound. The role of a CEO would be to harness and direct this flow.

This view is reflected by Peter Senge in his book *The Dance of Change*,[2] where he writes:

> In today's organizations, this idealization of great leadership leads to an endless search for heroic figures who can come in to rescue the rest of us from recalcitrant, non-competitive institutions. But might this very thinking be a key reason such institutions prevail? Might not the continual search for the hero-leader be a critical factor in itself, diverting our attention away from building institutions that, by their very nature, continually adapt and reinvent themselves, with leadership coming from many people in many places, not just from the top?

An organization of self-leaders will not suffer from this. People who are willing to take the lead and work at the leading edge of their competence do not need the protection of a hero-leader, who can be worshipped when things are going well and blamed when they go badly. They are willing to share the risks of creating organizations that are adaptable and capable of reinventing themselves. They create what Senge refers to as 'leadership communities'.

## INNER LEADERSHIP

*REAL personal transformation*

The context for inner leadership is to be able to take the lead and act more effectively within your organization. If this book does not enhance your effectiveness in the outside world, it has not succeeded. It will help you to adapt your behavior and act in the way you desire to act, consciously.

Inner leadership's systematic process for personal transformation contains the following elements (see Figure 1):

Figure 1  The inner leadership model

- Recognizing – increasing our self-awareness of our inner world and our qualities, recognizing aspects of ourselves of which we are relatively unaware.

- Exploring – learning more deeply who we are and how we limit ourselves through our assumptions, our beliefs and the various conflicting parts of our personalities.

- Actualizing – freeing ourselves from our habitual mindsets, constituents and behaviors to make conscious choices and to become integrated and autonomous people acting in accordance with our values and purpose.

- Leading – using our awareness and will to realize our deepest resources and self-leading potential. By seeing the real needs of each situation, we transform our own relationship to it and are able to respond with awareness, aptitude and purpose.

Inner leadership requires us to work on ourselves, but not just for our own sake. It is only worthwhile if it can be applied. One person realizing their self-leading potentiality will have an influence on the people around them. Many self-leaders give rise to an exponential multiplier effect.

**THE MULTIPLIER EFFECT**

People who have individually practiced the principles of inner leadership create high-performance teams when they come together. They are able to speak to each other with a high level of honesty and openness, they build trust easily and they tend not to be defensive. When we feel more secure in ourselves, we are able to risk expressing what we are thinking and feeling. We can take the risk of proposing a creative idea and not feel defeated if the idea is not taken on in its entirety. As a team we are more likely to build ideas between us, because hanging on to our own ideas is less important. The views of others are less likely to be seen as a threat. We take responsibility for our own views and responses and project less of our own feelings on to others.

In contrast, when we are defending ourselves against perceived attack, against looking stupid, against being wrong, we tend to blame other people and external factors for anything that goes wrong. When we do this we do not communicate clearly and, because problems are not owned but externalized or projected on to others, we do not have the opportunity to learn from our mistakes.

Case notes 1 describes the effect on a company where a number of people were practicing the principles of inner leadership. It describes, in this context, the main parts of the inner leadership process that are explained in more detail in the remainder of this book.

---

## CASE NOTES 1 – CORPORATE TRANSFORMATION BY SELF-LEADING

GCV was a small speciality chemicals research company within a large group. In 1989 it was close to completing the development of a new chemical, HZK, which was a potential blockbuster, far in advance of the competition technologically and with a wide range of applications. To fulfill this potential the company needed to be much larger.

The challenge for the company's CEO, Andrew, was to transform GCV from a small, loose, informal, science-led company into a highly professional and commercial research facility, in order to exploit HZK's potential. This was the purpose into which he decided to invest all his efforts.

The company needed to grow to a targeted 500 people. This would require 80 people to be recruited each year for the following four years, as well as an infrastructure capable of supporting them so that they could be productive. Andrew described the situation as transforming the company from 'being a small sailing dinghy which stays close to the shoreline into a large, ocean-going yacht'.

GCV did not have formal management apart from Andrew. Its top scientists became managers and directed the research, but their judgment was clouded by the fact that they each had their own areas of scientific interest and their favorite projects to which they were heavily attached. General company matters were only dealt with when they had an impact on the research.

Andrew was a scientist, with a PhD. He recognized that it was vital to develop GCV's people as leaders and managers in order to achieve the company's aims. He knew that to transform the organization he needed to transform the people first. He described the senior staff as being stuck in a university-type culture, arrogant in their knowledge and introspective. They were often more interested in the compounds and the science than in their applications.

Andrew had recently been through a difficult period in his life, which had caused him to question his view of himself and the world. This opened his eyes to see the problem the company faced in an interesting way. He recognized that many of the people working there, who had been academically very successful, had been

*A crisis breaks the mold*

cosseted in an academic world where stark reality rarely broke through. He said it was as if these people had never suffered the discomfort or pain it sometimes takes to make one question oneself. He knew that to transform the organization would be painful and challenging for many people, but unless this was done GCV would not succeed and fulfill its potential. Andrew was prepared to take people out of their comfort zones by bringing in a new reality.

At an initial meeting to discuss change within GCV, Andrew described a vision of the new organization he had formed with two other members of the management committee. Unfortunately, he presented this as a *fait accompli*. When he had finished, no one spoke for five minutes.

Then there was an outburst of angry discussion. The people who had not been consulted were furious. The meeting split into factions and fragments. By the end of the day there was confusion and conflict. Andrew could see his vision for the company disappearing.

Andrew's intentions had been good and he had been doing what he felt was genuinely right, but it had all backfired and the company was in a state of disarray. He did not know what to do now. He felt that people would lose faith in him if he backed down, and anyway he would find that a difficult thing to do. Part of him found it very difficult to admit that he was wrong. Part of him knew that he had to back down and apologise, but this would be painful for his self-image.

**LEADING WITH VALUES**

The following morning Andrew looked pale and exhausted. He had wrestled all night with his pride, his need to be right and acknowledging his error. He stood up in front of a hushed meeting and told those present that he had just been through the worst night of his life. He explained that he had thought he was acting in the company's best interests, but he had made a dreadful mistake in the way he had behaved. It was wrong of him to have planned this new organization in secret. He had tears in his eyes as he told the meeting that he did not want the company to be one where decisions are made behind closed doors, with no transparency and accountability. He genuinely felt this. If his managers considered that their trust in him was broken, he would resign.

The atmosphere in the room was tremendous. The meeting applauded him. This was a turning point. Andrew's qualities of courage and self-honesty set new values and standards for the company and for the work ahead to transform it. It provided a platform from which to change a mindset that had been limiting the company's ability to change. It said: 'We can learn from our mistakes by being open and honest, and we can forgive each other. We are all in this together.' From that moment, most of the managers in the group were behind the transformation. Those who were not realized the strength of others' commitment and, if they felt they could not go along with it for their own reasons, they soon left.

Each manager was assigned an individual coach who worked with them on the changes they needed to make in order to transform the company. It was important for them to look at themselves, at their initial reactions to the challenge before them, and to recognize their level of willingness in relation to this. These people were going to have to devote at least half of their time to management issues and, by implication, spend less time on their beloved science. They had to put the company first and their purpose became to grow and strengthen it enough to support the new product. In the same way that they had trained to be physicians, PhDs and specialists in their scientific fields, now they had to learn to lead and

RECOGNIZING

EXPLORING

manage people and they had to learn about themselves in relation to change and uncertainty. For most of them, this represented a huge change in role. They needed to understand that this would be personally challenging, and it would require a strong commitment and time.

Through this work, over a period of six months, the managers learned about personal transformation. Specifically, they learned about remaining open and honest to the task and among themselves, about being vulnerable, about managing their own fears and anxieties, about their individual mindsets and constituents. One particularly prevalent constituent was the empirical scientist, which came up in various shapes and forms. For many this was a block on action, experienced through a need for the certainty of facts and figures.

For example, Len ran the safety side of the company, an extremely important function collecting and organizing the necessary information to present to the safety authorities. Without this, no new products would reach the market. The work took great precision. There was no room for compromise or error. But in his work to transform the organization, Len had to let go of much of his training and enter a world where chaos would be created as the organizational structure and philosophy changed. The dictum was to make decisions that were 80 percent right rather than delay taking actions, then to be open to change the decisions if necessary.

In his coaching sessions it was obvious Len was going to struggle with this. It caused him a great amount of stress and angst to make these 80 percent accurate decisions. He stuck to the task, because he came to realize that his resistance was as a result of his identification with the safety expert and scientist within him. He knew this was not the only person he was and he recognized how important it was to him that the company could be transformed. This sense of purpose moved his choice from one of compromising between scientific rigor and 80/20 accuracy, which he saw to be 'inaccuracy', to being able to choose to make decisions that were timely and 'good enough'. With support and greater self-awareness, Len gradually became more comfortable with working in this way, and remained an important member of the management team.

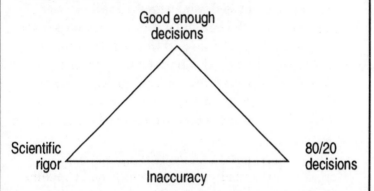

Throughout this time, keeping in mind the purpose and the values of the company helped most people to undertake this difficult work. The purpose and values bound them together, giving them the will not to give up during tough times. The basic values were openness, trust and honesty, and the purpose was very focused on bringing HZK to the market and creating an organization capable of supporting it and producing other valuable chemicals.

*Purpose and values*

As the members of the management team continued with this work on *personal* transformation, they gained a greater understanding of the process of *corporate* transformation. They came to understand what other people in the organization needed to help them implement changes. They changed their behaviors and made decisions based on what they saw, in the

**ACTUALIZING**

light of their values and purpose. One manager reflected:

> Doing this work took me to a very uncomfortable place. I started to think about the value I actually provided to the company. In this time of change and uncertainty, I began to wonder if I had it in me to see the changes through, to be a part of this new, emerging company. And I then realized, if I am having these thoughts, how must the people in my department feel, who have not had the benefit of the view of the transformation I have, or the benefit of the coaching and training? Suddenly my heart went out to those people and I knew I had to work with them to help them through the process. I had never felt like this before. I decided I must devote most of my time to working with the people.

**LEADING**

After six months the managers were brought together for a workshop to review the progress of the transformation and to plan the next stages. The change in their way of being together was remarkable.

People felt self-confident enough to stand by their own views and to listen to others. They were able to work together and give honest and valuable feedback. They were able to accept their own mistakes and those of others and learn from them to provide creative solutions to problems. Nothing was swept under the carpet. There was no shame in having limitations. It was a case of playing to people's strengths and supporting them where they were weak.

They were developing a belief that they could trust each other and work together to make the changes necessary to achieve the corporate transformation. They had become a team of self-leaders, with the individual and collective will to develop and transform themselves and the company.

The managers found that they had the tools to develop a broad strategy for the company based on a strong vision of where they wanted to be in five years' time. They were now able to look at possibilities based on their hunches and the rapidly changing reality they saw, knowing that things would not turn out exactly as expected, whereas before they had been paralysed by their need for scientific certainty. Now they are able to adapt their strategies without getting caught up in being wrong, or blaming.

The culture of transformation and change created in GCV was deepened by providing coaching and leadership programs to people coming in to the organization as it expanded, and to more of the existing people. I spoke to two recently who remembered this work as the most important they have done in terms of their leadership development and remarked that it still has an effect on how they are in the organization more than five years after the work was done.

In 1989 GCV employed fewer than 100 people. By 1993 it had reached its target of 400 people and developed HZK to be the leading drug in its field. In 1999 the company employed 1600 people, having used the money from HZK to develop a pipeline of new chemicals.

The greater number of projects meant that they had to transform their way of working from a line-based structure to being project led, which took another fundamental shift in thinking and working practices. But the attitudes and qualities necessary for change management were now available to cope with this. Through its individuals, GCV transformed itself into a professionally run and organized company without squeezing out individual entrepreneurship and creativity.

The case of GCV shows what can be achieved when self-leaders are widely developed in a company. This work is transformative at a personal level, recognizing the qualities and the diversity each holds, putting people in touch with a deeper level of understanding and inner resources, and giving them a new language to make the corporate transformation. Those with this experience, as they move around a company, reach higher positions or move to other companies, spread their ways of working and thinking far and wide. There are now people who worked in GCV in many other parts of the group, introducing still other people to it. It has become a part of the culture.

## Exercise 1
## Your purpose for inner leadership

What is your purpose for wanting to know more about inner leadership? How do you want to apply it in your life? Write down this purpose. Refer to it whenever you start your inner leadership sessions, and keep refining it or adapting it, if you want to, as you learn more. It is important to do this. It will keep you focused, provide you with motivation and give you a context for the work you do.

### USING THIS BOOK

I recommend that you read the whole book through once, as rapidly as you can. This will give you an overview. Don't worry about understanding all the details. Just allow the book to wash over you and trust yourself to take in all you need at this stage. This will prepare you for working through the book in detail, more slowly and doing as many of the exercises as you are willing to do.

You will find it helpful if you keep a journal in which you can write your thoughts, ideas and the exercises, so that you can easily refer back to them. You will learn a great deal about yourself. It is easy to forget the differences you will find in yourself, so a journal will also provide you with reference points. You will then have a complete record of the work you have undertaken.

*Inner Leadership* is set out in four main stages. Each will have an effect on you, so you don't have to wait to the end of the book to reap some benefits. This is illustrated in Table 1.

The inner leadership model is a spiral. I remember going on a train through the Rocky Mountains in Canada. The train climbed several thousand feet, in a spiral. As I looked out of the window I saw the same scenes come around again, but I was on a different level. This is what working through this book will be like. As you become more aware you will see patterns emerging, like familiar scenery, but you will never be observing it from the same place twice.

Inner leadership is a process to use and apply in the area of your choice. There is no finite end point to reach. I hope you will want to carry on using what you learn in the book, and keep referring back to it.

If you can put some regular time aside to go through your intentions, as though you were embarking on an external training course, that would be helpful.

If you can find another person who also wants to read *Inner Leadership*, you would benefit by meeting and discussing your experiences, supporting each other, providing a framework of time and effort and bouncing ideas between you. If you cannot find anyone, send me an email through the website **www.inner-leadership.com** and I will try to match you up with someone or find some other way to support you.

As a part of the practical application of this book, I encourage people to share their experiences. Visiting the website is also a good way to keep in touch with developments. This is a forum to talk to me and to each other, to support and inspire each other and to swap stories and ideas. There is a quarterly magazine and details of inner leadership courses, events and news.

## Table 1  The stages of inner leadership

| | Content | Benefits |
|---|---|---|
| *Recognizing* *(Chapters 2–3)* | Your physical reactions, emotions and thoughts<br>Your reactions and responses<br>How you view yourself<br>Changing behavior through awareness<br>Developing qualities | More realistic self-assessment<br>Being less reactive, more responsive<br>Seeing your qualities<br>Developing qualities you want<br>Making more informed choices<br>Defining who you want to be |
| *Exploring* *(Chapters 4–8)* | How we become who we are<br>Your defenses against anxiety<br>Your constituents<br>Your beliefs and expectations<br>Your mindsets<br>Your concept of yourself<br>Seeing unconscious factors that influence you<br>Your values and purpose | Deeper self-awareness<br>Greater freedom to choose<br>Seeing the influence of constituents and mindsets<br>Increased motivation and clarity<br>Reduced internal conflict<br>Defining who you want to be<br>Clarity of focus on your values and purpose |
| *Actualizing* *(Chapters 9–13)* | How we change<br>Your center of identity<br>Freeing yourself from habitual patterns<br>A realistic self-concept<br>Intensify and use your will<br>Accept yourself for who you are<br>Changing attitudes and behaviors | See situations clearly<br>Respond to real needs<br>Freedom to choose and act<br>Ability to change by adapting your self-concept<br>Working with contradictions and conflict<br>Deeper understanding of others<br>Greater self-confidence<br>Stronger resolve and flexibility |
| *Leading* *(Chapters 14–15)* | See clearly, act with aptitude<br>Transforming situations<br>Practicing inner leadership<br>Transforming inner leadership into leadership | Personal transformation<br>Achievement of your chosen purpose<br>Inspire loyalty and confidence<br>Be happy with yourself<br>Unlock your creativity<br>Choose to take the lead |

Inner leadership will not conflict with any other leadership work you are doing or any theory of leadership you are using. It will enhance it, because its aim is to help you to realize your inherent self-leading potential and to apply it. Don't replace existing leadership programs, but excel at them with the power of inner leadership behind you.

# Stage 1
# Recognizing

L eading
A ctualizing
E xploring
R ECOGNIZING

## RECOGNIZING MORE OF OURSELVES

Most people are not very self-aware. Most people don't know themselves very deeply. Does that surprise you? Do you really know what drives you, or why sometimes you feel incredibly motivated and sometimes you don't? Why do you react to certain people and situations in particular ways? Why do you suddenly feel irritated for no conscious reason? Why do you sometimes feel invincible and at other times are rendered powerless? The reasons often lie below your everyday level of consciousness.

When you become aware of them you can work with them. 'Recognizing' will increase your awareness of yourself. You will see more clearly the messages you can pick up from your physical reactions, your emotions and your thoughts (Chapter 2). You will come to know your qualities and their importance (Chapter 3).

Recognizing more of yourself will enable you to be more realistic about yourself, others and situations. It shows you more about yourself in a given moment, more than normally reaches your awareness. Because you will know where you stand, your self-confidence will rise. You will be standing on firm ground. You will become less reactive, able to make more informed choices and decisions and see the consequences of your actions more clearly.

# Recognizing Yourself   2

The process of recognizing enables you to observe closely your bodily reactions, emotions and thoughts in relation to a situation. By gaining a deep understanding and awareness of your body, emotions and thoughts, you can learn from them.

To be more effective, we need to make the most appropriate response to what is happening at that time. Response implies proactive choice, which is in contrast to reactiveness and passivity.

*Response over reaction*

For example, if you are feeling very annoyed with somebody, it is difficult to respond to them with understanding, to give them time to explain themselves or to remain open to new possibilities. You probably find it hard to look them in the eye. Your system is taken over by the annoyance and perhaps a tendency to blame the other person. At that moment you may hate them, or want to flee from them. It is even difficult to gauge whether your annoyance is justified. In this way we become reactive, rather than responsive. Our perspective is narrowed.

Your power to choose how you respond to events increases with self-awareness. To be responsive you need to know your starting point. You need to know what you are feeling and thinking.

## PHYSICAL REACTIONS

It is difficult to control your initial physical reactions to something. They tend not to lie. We may not always like what we feel, but it is not to be ignored. Lie detectors work on the principle of physical reactions. If something surprises you, your jaw may not fall open and your eyes bulge out, but you will feel some physical reaction.

*What's your body saying?*

Look out for tension, aches and pains, tiredness, butterflies in the stomach, crossed arms or legs, the depth of your breathing, changes in temperature, fidgeting, what you are doing with your hands, itchiness and other signs that will tell you whether you are in a general state of comfort or discomfort.

If you want to learn more about what physical reactions mean, buy a book on body language, of which there are several on the market. Most people buy them to find out what other people are thinking or feeling, but you can use them to discover what your own unconscious self is telling you.

## EMOTIONS AS A BAROMETER

Emotions are often misunderstood. People tend to focus on the 'negative' ones and see them as something to get rid of. The emotions are often glibly summarized as mad, sad, glad, bad and scared. Most of us don't mind being glad, but we certainly don't want to be any of the others.

This perception needs to be reframed. Our emotions are sources of information. They are a wonderful barometer for what is happening to us now. Being scared is a significant contributor to avoiding danger and staying alive. Sadness and anger show us what really matters to us, and therefore what we love, what we have a passion for, what we see as injustice. If we can observe our emotions and value them, instead of suppressing them, then they become our allies.

EMOTIONAL BAROMETER

Make a list of emotions you feel in your life. Then see Table 2 for a list of emotions. Are there more than you wrote down? Are there some that you don't allow yourself or don't want to feel? Perhaps your emotions are something to which you don't pay too much regard.

I remember being with a venture capitalist when we found out we were in stiff competition to win a bid. I asked him how he felt about it. Looking irritated and worried, he replied: 'I don't feel anything – it's just something else I have to deal with.' His feelings became visible, but he was neither in contact with them nor did he realize they were important.

## Table 2  Emotions

**Anger**: irritation annoyance fury outrage resentment exasperation indignation animosity hostility violence protectiveness rage

**Sadness**: unhappiness disappointment despondency hurt grief loneliness despair depression dejection self-pity gloom

**Enjoyment**: pleasure happiness joy delight effervescence comfort exhilaration excitement contentment relief pride thrill rapture gratification satisfaction euphoria

**Fear**: anxiety worry concern nervousness inhibition uncertainty dread fright terror panic consternation

**Shame**: guilt frustration embarrassment defeat remorse humiliation mortification envy

**Disgust**: contempt disdain scorn distaste revulsion aversion

**Surprise**: shock astonishment amazement wonder awe

**Love**: acceptance respect friendliness trust kindness devotion adoration infatuation jealousy

We are taught to pay most attention to our thinking, so we may feel we have more control over this. Try the following and see if you have.

Close your eyes. Imagine a white circle with a red disk in the center. Hold the disk still for 15 seconds.

How did you get on?

When faced with a stimulus or situation, our first thought is not under our control. It is hard to change, even if you can identify it before other thoughts come rushing in. Most of us employ very efficient internal editors that block unwelcome thoughts from our consciousness. Allow that editor to miss a few, even to take some time off. Exercise 2 will expand your self-awareness.

# Exercise 2 – Basic self-awareness

*You have no control over others, only over your own responses.*

Take a couple of minutes to reflect on that statement. Look for what is happening in your body, your emotions and your thoughts before you go any further.

How did reading the statement affect you? Consider whether your main reaction could be felt in your body, in your emotions or in your thoughts.

Did you have any physical response, such as a tensing of the muscles, a frown, butterflies in the stomach, or perhaps a rising energy up through your heart to your throat? Did you utter a sound, a sigh, a sucking in of breath, or did your eyes widen or narrow slightly? Did you move position in your chair, or cross your legs or your arms? How strong is that physical response if you really look at it, and what might it be telling you? What does it say about whether or not you liked the statement?

Did you feel any emotional response, however slight, such as irritation, powerlessness, exhilaration, panic, or even numbness? What is that telling you about how comfortable you felt with the statement?

How did your mind react to the statement? Did you think 'how ridiculous', or 'bunkum', or something stronger? Did you think 'how exciting', or 'how true', or did your mind go blank? Did you focus on how limited you feel or on the power you have to choose? What is this telling you about whether the statement fits in with your own deep beliefs, and therefore what your beliefs are?

Stopping for a moment and noticing what is happening within you allows you to gather a great deal of information about yourself.

---

What did you notice? If your reaction was strong, was it appropriately strong or was it a reaction because the statement threatened the way you normally think about things? Perhaps it was a defensive reaction.

Which of the following statements best fits your reaction?

- I found the statement exhilarating.
- I found the statement depressing.
- I found the statement irritating.
- I found the statement threatening.
- I found the statement astonishing.
- I found the statement embarrassing.
- I found the statement abhorrent.
- I found the statement comforting.

Or perhaps for you it was more than one of these, or something else. Write it down. The point is, if you observe yourself, there was probably more happening than you recognized at first.

## THE BENEFITS OF SELF-OBSERVATION

This exercise should have given you a glimpse of what you are capable of observing about yourself when you are awake to it. It shows you how your body, emotions and thoughts work together, giving both an integrated experience of yourself and a distinct experience of your different parts. You are both the one, a whole being, and the many parts. Perhaps you noticed that you were more attuned to one of the three areas, finding it difficult to believe the messages of the others.

*Early warning system*

That simple exercise can be applied to give you more information about your response to any situation. It is the basis for your being able to trust your own observations, your own feelings and your own thoughts. This self-observation will give you early warning of when you have an internal conflict, or when you are trying to tell yourself something.

Imagine you are in an important meeting about collaboration with another organization. Everyone seems friendly and things appear to be proceeding reasonably smoothly. You stop for a moment. Your legs are tightly crossed. Your hands are clammy and your stomach is churning. You feel irritable. In fact, if you take note of your emotions, you can feel a mild state of panic. Something is bothering you.

Wouldn't you decide to review what is happening more closely? Perhaps you really don't trust the other organization, or the people you are dealing with, or you could feel suspicious about their sales forecast, or you may be selling your side short in the negotiations. Whatever it is, you are now on full alert. You are aware of what had been stirring just below the normal level of your consciousness and you have the choice of whether to act on it.

## RECOGNIZING AS A PRECURSOR TO CHANGE

Recognizing keeps us in touch with deeper parts of ourselves. In this way, we are able to use a level of knowledge, insight and energy that rarely comes to the fore. In his book *Emotional Intelligence*, Daniel Goleman states:

> Self-awareness – recognizing a feeling as it happens – is the keystone of emotional intelligence. The ability to monitor feelings from moment to moment is crucial to

psychological insight and self-understanding. An inability to notice our true feelings leaves us at their mercy. People with greater certainty about their feelings are better pilots of their lives, having a surer sense of how they feel about personal decisions, from whom to marry to what job to take.[1]

---

## CASE NOTES 2 – CHANGING BEHAVIOR

Philip has recently been promoted to be technical director of a company running state-of-the-art manufacturing plants with turnover in excess of £100 million. He is in his mid-forties and is very well qualified for the job. However, he feels that his ideas are not taken up by his boardroom colleagues, even though they are often well considered and relevant.

For example, the company was in the process of setting up a new plant in Turkey. He had made an assessment of the situation and had concluded that it was very important not to replicate some of the engineering at the previous plant the company had set up in France, but he was not being heard. If they got this wrong, it could cost the company several million pounds in lost sales and delays.

In working with Philip as his inner leadership mentor, I listened to him talk about this. I experienced what happens when he is putting forward his views. He becomes attached to his ideas and dismissive of everything else. It is difficult to interrupt his flow. His face looks set and he points and wags his finger. He comes over as being a mixture of overly aggressive and 'holier-than-thou', what he came to call his evangelist constituent.

One day when he did this I reacted to him in the way I felt his colleagues would feel. My body language showed I was wanting to back away from him. I became dismissive and defensive. Through working with this process he was able to see the effect he was having.

By practicing the self-awareness exercise he recognized how tense he feels when he has to put his point of view over. His legs are tightly crossed, his shoulders are high, the muscles around his mouth are tight. His main emotions are anxiety and isolation. His initial thought about himself is that he will not be heard, that people are not interested in what he says.

He behaves in this way because it is how he feels inside, because he believes that people will not hear what he has to say unless he is totally convincing and speaks vehemently. As the youngest of five children, in a family who argued a great deal, he had learned to put his views uncompromisingly in order to be heard. In his current situation this was no longer appropriate.

By recognizing his physical reactions, emotions and thoughts, he can now monitor himself more effectively. Encouraged by his ability to see himself, he practiced different behaviors, subtler and gentler ways of persuasion. He practiced feeling calmer within himself. He learned not to personalize his comments about the causes of the problems he was now trying to solve and not to blame others in order to feel better himself.

This change in approach had an immediate effect on his relationship with his colleagues and how his proposals were received. He used his new behavior to turn things around and persuade his colleagues to change the way the new plant was set up, avoiding a potentially costly mistake and so improving the company's performance.

If you are willing, do the following exercise. I ask if you are willing because I want you to think about where you stand in relation to the work you are doing with this book. How willing are you? What makes you feel more or less willing? Keep in mind Exercise 1 at the end of Chapter 1, establishing your purpose for working through this book.

## Exercise 3 – Using your self-awareness

Next time you are in an important meeting with someone, or undertaking a serious task, or making a vital decision, remember to stop for a moment and recognize what is happening to you.

- What are your physical sensations?
- What are your emotions?
- What are your initial thoughts?
- What does this information tell you about yourself in relation to the person, the situation or the task?
- Does this information have any bearing on how you behave or the decisions you make?

Write up your reactions afterwards.

How might increased self-awareness help you to be a self-leader and take the lead? How do you think it could affect you in your decision making, your work relationships and your dealings with customers or suppliers?  Make some notes on these aspects.

# 3 Recognizing Your Qualities

THE AIM OF RECOGNIZING YOUR QUALITIES

In this chapter you will look beyond your everyday skills into the deeper qualities you have, so that you can access them. Qualities are your most important resource because they create a platform from which you can become a self-leader.

Attitudes are the basis of how we think and, with effort, can be changed. Skills are the basis of what we do and can be acquired through training. Knowledge can be learned. But qualities are the basis of who we are and how we conduct ourselves.

It is very common for people to be unaware of their qualities. We are more likely to know our specific skills. Few of us really think deeply about ourselves in relation to what we want to achieve in life or what our roles demand of us and which qualities would be the most helpful.

*Inner Leadership* is more concerned with putting you in touch with your qualities than your skills, because a quality is associated with the nature, characteristic, attribute or worth of something. Think of the purpose you have set yourself in learning about inner leadership and about how recognizing your qualities could help you to achieve that.

## Exercise 4 – Recognizing your qualities

Consider the qualities in the three columns overleaf. On the grid that follows, plot each quality using its abbreviation, according to the following two coordinates:

- The extent to which you consider that the quality is present in yourself.
- The extent to which you believe that the quality is important in your work/life.

Each category should be plotted according to the following scoring system:

1 = never present/not at all important
5 = sometimes present/quite important
10 = always present/very important

Don't worry about plotting categories to the highest degree of accuracy, but get them into the right area. Plot each column in a different color.

The qualities used in the exercise can be subjectively defined. If you see autonomy as the ability to stand for what you believe in and take the initiative, you may give it a high score in terms of importance. If you see autonomy as the inability to be a member of a team, you may score it low in terms of importance. As long as you know why you have put the quality in a certain place, that is good enough.

Not all these qualities are what most people would deem to be positive, but qualities in themselves are all neutral. Their relevance depends on the circumstances in which they are used. Autocracy can sometimes be effective and open-mindedness can sometimes be a hindrance. The objective of the exercise is for you to think about these qualities and the extent to which you feel you have them and how important they are to your role. This is not a test and there are no right or wrong answers.

Each column contains different types of qualities. That is why it is useful to plot each in a different color, in order to give you a quick overall view when you study your completed sheet. Do this without judging yourself. This exercise is partly about how honest and how accepting you can be about yourself. If you wish, add some other qualities of your choice to the list.

| COLOR 1 | COLOR 2 | COLOR 3 |
| --- | --- | --- |
| autocracy (au) | direction (dr) | self-awareness (sa) |
| decisiveness (dc) | support (sp) | open-mindedness (om) |
| control (ct) | information sharing (is) | purpose (pp) |
| single-mindedness (sg) | motivation (mt) | value led (vl) |
| aggression (ag) | enthusiasm (en) | responsiveness (rp) |
| impatience (im) | fairness (fr) | respect (rc) |
| reactiveness (ra) | forgiveness (fg) | creativity (cr) |
| rationality (rt) | adaptability (ad) | humor (hm) |
| secrecy (sc) | criticism (cs) | trust (ts) |
| judgment (jg) | scepticism (st) | compassion (cp) |
| cynicism (cy) | efficiency (ef) | goodwill (gw) |
| organization (og) | understanding (us) | love (lv) |
| | independence (ip) | truth (tr) |
| | cooperation (co) | beauty (bt) |
| | leading by example (le) | |

Did anything about this exercise surprise you? How was it to do it? What feelings were evoked? Did you feel relaxed or tense? Did you enjoy it? Was it easy to stick to the task? What did your mind think of it all? Make a few notes on this.

The important thing about this exercise is to encourage you to recognize your qualities and compare them to those you think are most required to be effective and take the lead in your particular organization. Notice the categories you had difficulty placing. This is also valuable information about yourself.

You could do the exercise separately for work and non-work life and compare whether the qualities you display are different

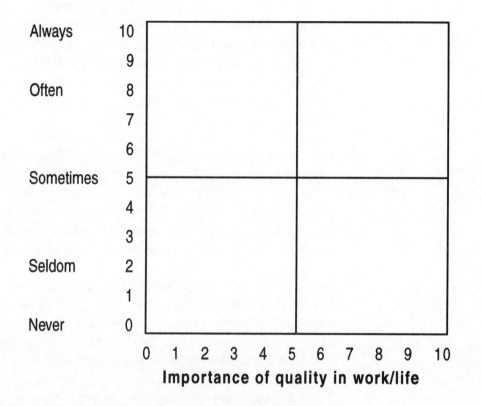

**Extent to which quality
is present in you**

| | |
|---|---|
| Always | 10 |
| | 9 |
| Often | 8 |
| | 7 |
| | 6 |
| Sometimes | 5 |
| | 4 |
| | 3 |
| Seldom | 2 |
| | 1 |
| Never | 0 |

0  1  2  3  4  5  6  7  8  9  10

**Importance of quality in work/life**

in each area. What does this say about your approach to work, or about what you allow yourself to be at work compared with other aspects of your life?

The left-hand column of the grid represents qualities on which many hierarchical organizations are based, though not all, of course. The middle column represents qualities of flexible organizations. In the right-hand column we have the qualities that inner leadership is likely to bring out in you. This is in my opinion, and I stress that qualities can be used differently in different settings, so there is no judgment implied.

*The bottom right quadrant* is the area where you believe the qualities to be important but feel you don't present them sufficiently. By looking at this area you will see the qualities you wish to develop.

*The top right quadrant* is the area that shows qualities that you believe you present and that you consider important. These are things you will want to keep honed and perhaps improve further.

*The top left quadrant* includes qualities that you present often but that are not very important in your role. These can be a pointer towards areas where you have a conflict, for example you may show compassion at work, where you believe it is not important or appropriate. Does this show a difference in values? Or perhaps you are making an assumption about what is allowable at work. Think about whether some of these qualities may be more appropriate than you first thought.

*The bottom left quadrant* contains aspects that are neither important nor used. Just make sure they really aren't important. All have their place somewhere, in some situation. There can be a tendency to downgrade the importance of things we feel we lack.

**WHAT DID YOU LEARN ABOUT YOURSELF?**

Now write up what you learned about yourself from the exercise. How might your view of the qualities you possess affect the way you behave in future? Perhaps you have opened up new areas of thinking about yourself. Make a list of those areas that you consider to be most important in taking the lead and working at your leading edge.

Are there any areas that are of immediate concern to you? Make a note of these. Perhaps there are some you wish to develop. Note them, but don't judge yourself. Where you are at the moment is fine.

Notice in your daily work the impact of having done this exercise. You may find you feel clearer about how to carry out your role. How does this color the responses you make? Are you seeing things differently in some areas? Perhaps your relationships with others are changing. Perhaps you feel more open to receive input from somebody else, or able to release some control. Do you find that people react to you any differently? Keep a note of any changes you notice.

Write down how what you have learned in this exercise helps you in your desire to be a self-leader.

**YOU HAVE ALL THE QUALITIES**

I believe that we all have the total spectrum of qualities within us, some of which are developed and some of which are relatively latent. This means that we all have the potential to be at both ends of the scale, for example both cynical and trusting. The aim is to develop the qualities we feel we need in order to make our lives what we want them to be. So even if you feel you don't have an ounce of some of the qualities you think you need in your life, you can develop them.

## Exercise 5 – Developing a quality

If you are willing, sit in a quiet place where you won't be disturbed with paper and a pencil handy. Take a few deep breaths and concentrate on your breathing for a minute or so, just noting its rise and fall, not trying to control it.

Think of the name of the quality you want to evoke in yourself, for example creativity. Reflect on this word. To you, what is its quality, its nature, its meaning? As thoughts and ideas come to you, write them down.

Keep thinking of the quality. What ideas and images emerge as you continue to reflect? See yourself with the quality. Think of a situation you are currently concerned about, or a situation in which you often find yourself. How would you behave if you were practicing this quality? What would your attitudes be? Would you look different in any way? Would you sound different? Perhaps you feel there is somebody, or something, that embodies that quality. Continue to write what comes to you.

Think of the quality in broader terms. How would it be helpful in your relationships, within your organization, in your family and in a broader world? Think of positive outcomes associated with this quality. Repeat the name of the quality several times. Tell yourself you want it to be a greater part of your life.

You will now have a feeling of what it is like to have developed this quality within yourself. Try to keep this feeling as you approach situations that require it. See and feel yourself with the quality. It will be present if you want it.

Write the word down somewhere you will see it several times a day. When you see it, recall the feeling you associate with the quality. This will strengthen it every time you do this.

Do this for each of the qualities you want to develop as a self leader, practicing inner leadership.

Don't attempt to 'undevelop' qualities you want to display less. By developing those you want, you will naturally replace the others.

# *Stage 2*
# *Exploring*

L eading
A ctualizing
E XPLORING
R ecognizing

Having been through the initial process of raising aspects of your self-awareness, Stage 2, Exploring, will deepen the process of knowing yourself.

Heightening your knowledge of yourself and gaining a more realistic self-concept gives you the clarity to respond to the real needs of new situations. In working with people in companies, I find how important it is to be able to take a 'reality check', to make sure the filter of assumptions and attitudes through which we see events is as clear as possible. Max De Pree, retired chief executive of furniture company Herman Miller, wrote in his book *Leadership is an Art*: 'The first task of a leader is to help define reality.'[1] In order to be able to do that, you first have to see your own reality as clearly as possible.

**CONSTITUENTS AND MINDSETS**

> We all like to believe we make decisions rationally and objectively. But the fact is we all carry biases, and those biases influence the choices we make.
>
> Hammond, Keeney and Raiffa
> *Smart Choices: A Practical Guide to Making Better Decisions*[2]

Exploring will deepen your awareness and experience of your constituents. It will deepen your perception and understanding of your own self-image, your beliefs and expectations, attitudes and assumptions, which are your mindsets. Constituents are covered in Chapter 5 and mindsets in Chapter 6. Chapter 4 explains how they form.

**VALUES AND PURPOSE**

Each of us holds fundamental values and a purpose, which often become buried in the busyness of everyday life. Values are a vital ingredient for both personal and corporate success. They provide a framework for decision making and for our behaviors. Purpose provides direction and focus for everything we do. In this stage you will explore your values and your purpose, in Chapters 7 and 8.

# *How We Become Who We Are*  4

## FORMING OUR OWN REALITY

Our view of reality is colored by our life experiences and the messages we receive from outside ourselves, particularly from our parents and other important figures, and our social environment. Childhood experiences have an especially strong impact, because we are then at our most impressionable and vulnerable.

Psychological development depends on crossing thresholds safely, which itself depends on the quality of care we receive and the extent to which we have the freedom to develop as ourselves. When put under pressure, or when certain experiences are reenacted, we tend to experience the feelings we have had before, perhaps as children. This is why you sometimes see people react to events seemingly inappropriately, perhaps becoming very angry or breaking down in tears of self-loathing and remorse.

I have seen this happen in dozens of cases through my career, where senior executives throw tantrums and intimidate anyone who expresses a contrary opinion. Peter Senge notes this in *The Dance of Change*.[1] He talks of the

CEO who thinks he gets on well with his fellow executives, but if you talk to them:

> they are terrified of him. If they speak of any significant change, or confront him with bad news, he'll launch into a tirade or humiliate them before the group. Since they can't be direct with him they scheme, flatter and manipulate the situation to try and get the boss to do what they want.

Consequently, the CEO's view of the world remains unchallenged, and he does not receive the information he needs to make the best decisions.

We have all been anxious at various points in our lives. As a child our anxiety may be about survival or discomfort. Later in life it may be about security (which could come out in issues like housing or money), isolation (relationships, love or family), meaninglessness (purpose, values or roles) or death (mortality, illness, pain or change). These are the existential issues with which all of us deal. But our anxiety can also be about freedom, responsibility or development, or about fulfilling our potential and being who we truly are.

It is easy to think that we do not achieve all we want, or allow ourselves to be who we are, because we are frightened of failing. But we can be as frightened of our power and success as we are of failure. Nelson Mandela recognized this in his inaugural speech on being made President of South Africa in 1994:

> Our deepest fear is not that we are inadequate. Our deepest fear is that we are powerful beyond measure. It is our light, not our darkness, that most frightens us. We ask ourselves, who am I to be brilliant, gorgeous, talented and fabulous?  Actually, who are you not to be? ... As we let our light shine, we unconsciously give other people permission to do the same. As we are liberated from our own fear, our presence automatically liberates others.

Many people suppress parts of themselves in order to be acceptable, finding ways of flattening out their feelings through drugs, alcohol or work, or being overly immodest and unassuming, or not wanting to stand out from the crowd or show others up, or setting their sights too low and not trying to fulfill their potential.

We are complex beings, the products of the sum of our experiences as well as our gene pools. There is a continual tension between the pull to grow and develop as people and the status quo, between expressing our uniqueness and conforming, between allowing ourselves to live freely and reigning ourselves in. We learn to defend ourselves against these tensions, or conflicts, by driving into the unconscious parts of ourselves, parts of our uniqueness, our aspirations, the parts of ourselves we don't like or find it difficult to accept, or those we think others may find it difficult to accept.

*Status quo vs personal growth*

All our parts seek expression, and those we repress don't die but find ways of living of which we are unaware. In this way they control us, and this is why self-exploration is such an important aspect of inner leadership.

## OUR CONSTITUENTS

We unconsciously develop aspects of ourselves in response to experiences and conditions in our lives. When these parts of ourselves become semipermanent and relatively autonomous regions of our personality, capable of acting as a separate person, we call them constituents. They are capable of dominating our behavior, our decisions and our reactions to events. Examples of constituents include the martyr, the controller, the idealist, the persecutor, the rebel and the victim. They can be identified by looking at our relatively fixed reactions and patterns of behavior.

*Those who live within us*

As children and beyond into adulthood, we tend to do what we perceive is needed, what we believe is expected of us in order to survive, to be loved, to be popular, not to be abandoned and to avoid pain and anxiety. Many of these constituents center on what we think other people want us to be, and they reflect how we see ourselves.

For example, many successful people are driven by a requirement to achieve. This often comes from wanting to please our parents when we are young and is reinforced by society's values. Parents may praise for achievement, everything from getting your spoon in your mouth to academic results, and criticize failure, not always overtly but implicitly. In the world of a child, dependent on parents for survival, the message is that if we are to be loved and valued, and therefore not abandoned, we must conform to their rules. We may develop a pleasing, achieving constituent. But this is likely to find a counter balance, so we may also develop a secretive or rebellious 'bad' side.

When I was a child my behavior at home was excellent, but at school it was appalling. Unconsciously, I had neatly split my 'good' side and my 'bad' side. The 'bad' side often confirms to ourselves that we are not acceptable; the 'good' side is built up more to cover this.

## OUR MINDSETS

We also form mindsets as psychological defense mechanisms, which protect us from anxiety and make sense of the reality we encounter. To feel safe we need to make our world seem normal. Through our mindsets we may arrange our lives to keep the defense mechanisms in place and avoid things that cause us anxiety. This leads to habitual thought patterns, which are resistant to change.

*Mindsets as a filter*

Mindsets are the deep beliefs, attitudes, expectations, prejudices, views, self-concept and norms we hold about ourselves and the world. They fundamentally affect our decisions and our behaviors. Mindsets are a filter through which we see the world to help us cope with an ever-changing reality. We use them to screen out things we don't want to see and hear and to confirm what we do want to see and hear. Without mindsets, the incoming sensory, cognitive and emotional data could be overwhelming.

The problems arise, as with constituents, when we identify strongly with a few mindsets, so that we come to believe that we *are* them. They narrow our perspective when they become fixed and inflexible.

When you come to look at your mindsets in Chapter 6, you will see that some are very strong and go back a long way. Our fundamental mindsets are often formed in our early years and carry a strong emotional charge. So you may know you are dealing with a mindset when you find you feel strongly about something, when it seems particularly important to put over your view and defend it.

SEEING YOUR OWN REALITY

It is important to keep in mind that we live our lives under a number of assumptions, that there is more than one reality. When we can only see our own point of view, we are trying to impose a single reality.

The strength of these defense mechanisms is not to be underestimated. People can completely block traumatic events out of their memory, especially events from childhood. However, the repressed memory, now in the unconscious, will have a strong influence on that person's life, perhaps in the form of a fear, a phobia or a neurosis.

More routinely, we may use a set of beliefs to rationalize our own or others' behavior. When their self-esteem is low, many people find themselves using their mindsets, perhaps in the form of prejudices, to criticize other people and make themselves feel better. Someone who is anxious about failing, because 'failure is bad', may form a mindset of perfectionism as a reason not to start things at which they feel they may fail.

So we may tell ourselves that we are incapable of something or that we are not allowed to do it. We may repress thoughts or memories, or hear selectively. We may invalidate things that we or others have done, or belittle or inflate ourselves, or project our anxieties, hopes, shortcomings and competencies on to others. In these ways we construct our own reality and reinforce it over time. It is from this that we develop our strong traits, for example optimism or pessimism, introversion or extroversion, aggression or passiveness, trust or mistrust.

I remember an incident that exemplifies how we experience what we expect. I was to meet the wife of a colleague of mine. Her name was Claudette. She was one of 11 children from a Catholic family. I assumed that she was French. We met and had been talking for 10 minutes when I asked her where in France she came from. She laughed. At that moment I realized she had a Manchester accent, not a French one. Her name and the fact she was Catholic had completely blocked out what was really coming through to my senses. My impression dominated my real experience.

---

**CASE NOTES 3**
**SELF-AWARENESS ALLOWS CHANGE**

Greg held a particular mindset about himself. He said that he felt like a fraud, who would be exposed as being incompetent. At work he kept a low profile and was secretive. He spent a great deal of time making sure that what he did was as perfect as possible, and covering up any possible mistakes. Eventually, this took so much of his time that his work output declined.

His manager noticed this, and called him in to talk about it. Of course, now Greg felt that his incompetence had been exposed and his initial fear was confirmed, strengthening the mindset.

Greg had to work to expose this mindset as not being true and find a way to unlock himself from it. He found that it went back to a time when he had been humiliated at school by a teacher because he got flustered and could not recite his five times table one day. He was ridiculed for this by his classmates for a long time afterwards. After that, being wrong was almost unbearable to him and his confidence in his abilities remained insecure, giving rise to the feeling of being a fraud. His internal feeling of incompetence did not match the reality of the talents and qualities he possessed. He made sense of this by seeing himself as a fraud who sometimes showed talents that he did not really have, and whom he did not consider to be really Greg.

Holding himself back, because he had to do things 'perfectly', served him because it kept him away from risking new challenges, from the possibility of being wrong. It also confirmed to him that he could only be right by checking and double-checking his work.

Greg is an intelligent man with a high IQ and many good qualities. He has learned to break the connection between not being perfect and being a fraud. Over time he has learned not to undermine himself in this way. Now he is able to take more risks – to risk being wrong – which allows him to work more creatively and openly, bringing about a significant improvement in his output. In addition, he has become a good manager of other people, as a result of understanding himself and his own vulnerabilities. People working with him find his openness refreshing and tend to act in the same way themselves.

A simple occurrence, which at the time must have seemed innocuous to others, had a frighteningly significant effect on Greg's life. The traumatic event became buried in his unconscious and from there exerted a powerful influence over him that had a deep effect.

By working through this book and becoming aware of your own predominant mindsets and constituents, you will become able to broaden your self-image and respond to the reality of the situation, releasing energy bound up in any current conflict. It is like cleaning the filter through which we see things.

Through exploring, you will be able to peel away layers that will allow you to know who you really are and to understand more clearly what affects your decisions and behavior. Some of us have more layers than others. That is fine – it depends on our life experiences.

Being aware of the basic assumptions through which we see the world is important for our ability to change our behaviors and to respond to the real requirements of a situation. We need to understand that we are made up of many parts. We are influenced by our deep beliefs and the assumptions and the norms that we hold. These are critical to the choices and decisions we make and to our capacity to take on change.

## ADAPTING TO REALITY

Even when our circumstances change, our basic mindsets and dominant constituents often remain the same. They are slow to adapt, giving the status quo a strong hold. We build a wall between the mindset or constituent and reality. The more conflict there is between the two, the higher and thicker the wall becomes to stop reality breaking through and threatening the view we have of the world. We build certain aspects of ourselves and see the world relatively narrowly. Therefore we are not responding to the real needs of a situation or person with awareness and aptitude.

The effect of this can be seen in individuals and in organizations. It is becoming more and more accepted that change in organizations is slow because it is difficult for people to change. Michael Hammer and Steven Stanton, in *The Reengineering Revolution Handbook*, summed up their experience of working with hundreds of companies on reengineering projects by saying: 'The hardest part of reengineering is living through change, getting people to let go of their old ways and embrace the new ones.'[3] And they add with a hint of despair: 'The vagaries of human behavior seem infinitely more intricate than even the most complex processes.'

They are, and that is why they need more attention.

# *Exploring Your Constituents* 5

By exploring our constituents we come to appreciate the diversity that exists within each of us, a diversity that enables us to make our choices from a broad perspective and improves our ability to respond to the real needs of any situation. When we are dominated by a few constituents because we consciously or unconsciously identify with them, they direct our lives and reduce our breadth of choice.

## CASE NOTES 4 – 'POOR PENNY' ET AL.

This account was given to me by a woman to whom I gave a draft of this book while I was writing it. She is a partner in a major commercial law firm.

'I was reading a draft of your book at a time of considerable uncertainty in my life: I had just moved house and taken on a huge mortgage (a fivefold increase on my previous modest borrowings) to

*Change and uncertainty*

acquire an executive residence in the country – a big move for a country girl from Cumbria who had lived in London (thinking myself an "urban chick") for the best part of 20 years. I had been promoted rapidly, got some massive pay rises, and had set up a new team and then had to give it up to someone else's control as part of a big internal restructuring. I had some real problems getting my two young children into new schools and coping with the demands of homework, and having just "celebrated" my 39th birthday suddenly saw 40 looming fast.

*Self-doubt*

'Being seen to be both physically attractive and hugely financially successful has always been very important to me. I started to get very worried about my value to the organization in which I was a partner, whether my performance was justifying my pay packet, and whether I would keep earning the money to pay the big mortgage. Every conversation I had about my new role following the restructuring I interpreted as a veiled threat that my days in the firm were numbered. I also convinced myself that I was going gray too fast, and getting too old to wear the short skirts that showed off my legs (by now my only redeeming physical feature).

'I then read your book, and was particularly struck by the section on constituents. I recognized that I did indeed have many personalities and a particularly powerful one – which I nicknamed Poor Penny – was dominating my every thought and action. My demise was in serious danger of becoming a self-fulfilling prophecy, despite my track record and widely recognized intellectual and people skills, despite the reassurances of my friends and colleagues.

'I thought about my other constituents and recognized some others. One I call Joyce Grenfell – don't ask me why – she is amazingly brisk, capable, efficient, in control, organized, in fact a truly amazing woman. There's another one I call Brigitte Bardot – the has-been sex kitten. Another one I call Shirley Conran – superwoman.

'Having recognized this, it took about three seconds to see that neither Joyce nor Shirley would stand any nonsense from the Poor Pennys of this world, a rather pathetic individual who deserves everything she'll undoubtedly get; and they'd think that Brigitte is a bit dim, as well as being blind to the natural beauty and allure of her vitality and love of life (another constituent – I call her Mary Wesley).

'In summary, I have instructed Joyce and Shirley to tell Poor Penny to stop whinging, and every now and then I let Mary take the floor, for the sheer hell of it. Reading your draft has transformed what's going on in my head – and people have noticed. I have been offered four new roles in the restructured organization, as well as an unsolicited job offer from outside. I know exactly what I want to do – and I'm doing it. I am enjoying being alive and nearly 40 very much indeed.'

*Joyce Grenfell to the rescue*

In this case Penelope was able to see her behavior more clearly once she had been able to view herself in terms of being a number of constituents, none of which was entirely her. Note how the constituents are described as people, capable of becoming involved in different aspects of Penelope's life.

'Poor Penny' is vulnerable and insecure. She suffers low self-esteem and has been rejected because she does not fit with Penelope's self-image. She has become an unconscious and powerful part of Penelope, capable of determining her behavior and her feelings. She comes to the fore when Penelope feels uncertain, under pressure and vulnerable.

Penelope is driven to achieve, to be successful. Her description of herself as a 'country girl from Cumbria' suggests that she is involved in a world that is somewhat foreign to her, and to be successful she feels she has to be wily and tough. Her self-image therefore includes sexual attractiveness (Brigitte Bardot), brusque efficiency (Joyce Grenfell), power (Shirley Conran) and raw energy (Mary Wesley). Perhaps Poor Penny carries the quality of compassion that is needed to counter Penelope's harder edges. Poor Penny may become the precipitator of a change in Penelope that would bring her towards being a more integrated person, able to accept and access more parts of herself.

The message to Poor Penny is to say, 'Thank you – you have been useful – but I don't need you around so much now.' By seeing the quality of compassion in Poor Penny, Penelope may come to see a different role for her and value her more. This means that she does not need to consign Poor Penny to being a repressed part in the unconscious again. It is very important not to consign constituents to permanent exile.

## IDENTIFICATION

The problem that arises with constituents – and also with mindsets, explored in Chapter 6 – is that we come to identify ourselves with them. We identify with them to the extent that we think, at a given time, that they are all we are. We can be hijacked by them. We cannot see past them.

For example, we may identify with a temporary emotion or thought pattern, and lose or distort our perspective. Or we may become identified, as Penny's story shows, with a constituent, which follows a preprogrammed and predictable pattern of behavior when evoked by a certain set of circumstances. Therefore we are not free to choose how we act. Roberto Assagioli wrote:

> We are dominated by everything with which our self identifies. We can dominate, direct and utilize everything from which we can disidentify ourselves.[1]

In general, we tend to identify with whatever has the strongest pull, whatever we find most important or most stimulating, or whatever is protecting us from our greatest fears and anxieties. We identify with whatever fits best with our self-image, whatever motivates us to do things, or whatever fulfills our strongest desires, urges and needs.

In Case notes 1 in chapter 1, GCV, many of the senior managers identified with themselves as scientists, not as managers, or with their projects or with the science itself. If they had not been able to change these identifications, they would not have been able to come together and manage the growth of the company.

This process is often quite unconscious. Many people identify strongly with their physical body, as beautiful or ugly, fat or thin, fit or unfit. This turns into a problem when we become obsessed with comparing ourselves to the ideal body image perpetrated by the media and advertising. Others identify with their role, as an executive, a mother, an artist. Some identify with their psychological orientation, as an optimist or pessimist, free thinker or devil's advocate, controller or victim, happy or sad. Some identify with their qualifications, such as PhD, accountant or technical engineer. Some identify with their ideas. Some people identify with a group, like patriots with their national group, football supporters with their club.

We may become dependent on these aspects for our own sense of identity. If they are taken away from us, we may feel destroyed. If they are bestowed on us, we may feel enhanced. This is why some people feel so utterly devastated if they lose their job or role. They feel as if they are losing an integral part of themselves.

*We identify with where our energy goes*

## DEVELOPING CONSTITUENTS

It is as though we are a number of people living in the same house. Different parts can come to the fore at different times. Another way to look at them is as different instruments within an orchestra. They can come in at different points, and play loud or soft, fast or slow, but each has a sound, or a quality, which is unmistakeable.

Our constituents are part of the persona we use to face the world and protect ourselves. They are often polar

opposites. For example, many people who feel insecure have a strong, outward constituent to cover the insecure one. A tough person, capable of making unemotional decisions and firing staff without hesitation in the name of efficiency, may be soft-hearted outside the workplace, supporting local charities to help the community and running the junior football team.

John, a successful information technology consultant, developed a strong constituent he called Commander John, who was self-assured and confident to the point of being brusque. He liked to take control of situations. On the other hand John had another constituent, Little Jack, who was shy, timid and vulnerable. Little Jack rarely appeared, but in times of extreme stress John knew he was there.

Different constituents may coexist without mutual interference, but equally they may collide to cause internal conflict and feelings of guilt and ambivalence. Because we may believe that we should not have internal conflicts, or we find them uncomfortable, we expend energy keeping the contradictory factors apart. By driving them apart, they are unable to interact. If they could, some of the toughness could be applied to training the football team and some of the softer qualities could be applied in the workplace. As we have seen in the cases of Greg and Penelope, driving things into the unconscious gives them the power to control us.

Many constituents stem from what we think other people want us to be, but we come to believe that they are us. They also reflect how we see ourselves in relation to others and our environment.

In Case notes 1, Len did not realize the extent to which his safety officer constituent ruled his life until he explored it. Everything had to be ordered, rational and safe for him. People choose their roles for a reason. To Len, safety and security were issues in all aspects of his life. Moving away from this caused him internal conflicts that he found uncomfortable.

## CASE NOTES 5
## A CONSTITUENT'S DEVELOPMENT

Steve was the eldest of three children and the only male child in his family. His father was a top lawyer and let Steve know from an early stage that he expected great things of him. His mother shared ambitious feelings for him. They sent him to an expensive public school and provided extra tuition for him in his weaker subjects. He received approval and rewards for achievement, and criticism for failure. When things did not go well, he could feel his parents disappointment with him, which he interpreted as lack of approval.

Steve worked hard at school. He was good at sport and was in the top quartile in all classes, but he was always pushed to do better. He came to identify strongly with excelling at things. No matter how much he achieved, he never felt quite satisfied. He got into Oxford University and read law, like his father. He was disappointed to narrowly miss a first-class degree, but he obtained a graduate place in a top firm of lawyers. By the time he was 30, he was heading towards partnership. He was seen as the man for the grueling jobs in the corporate sector, often working punishing hours to complete a merger or takeover. He was still single, not having much time for relationships, and beginning to drink more heavily as a way to relax.

His constituent 'the Achiever' had many positive aspects. Steve developed into a person who could be trusted and he was fun to go sailing and rock climbing with, when he could spare the time. He was level headed and diligent, and he was confident and knew how to take the initiative. He could inspire others to work hard and was liked and respected by many people. He was an active member of his church and a godfather to two children. He was seen to be a very successful person.

*The constituent as the
center of the personality*

Early in his life, the Achiever became the central part of who Steve was. As he got older, it became the part around which many of the elements of his personality grew. Eventually, the Achiever became a complex psychological structure, which included a large number of personality elements and systems.

Of course, at this stage Steve was not even aware of the Achiever. It was the basis of his intellect, his determination, his group of friends and his view of life. Although it had helped him develop many valuable qualities – particularly valued by his parents, his colleagues and the society in which he functioned – he was no longer in control of it. The Achiever had become so dominant that Steve could not see beyond it. It was severely limiting him. Steve had forgotten what it was like to be intimate, to feel joy, to do something creative with his hands, to relax deeply, to read a book, to see beauty in things. Nevertheless, his urge for achievement had brought him so much of what he thought he should have. He assumed it was an intrinsic personality trait, and it was something of which he was proud.

Behind the Achiever lay a deep need, pushing to be recognized. That was for the approval and acceptance he had longed for as a child. As all children do, he had wanted love and affection without condition, just for being who he was. As a young boy, he had tried many ways to gain approval from his parents – being funny, helpful, endearing, helpless, good, ill. But none of them worked like achieving, like being the first of his age group to walk, to ride a bike. to get his swimming certificate. Consequently, another constituent, the Longing Child, had formed and had been repressed, because its qualities were incompatible with the stronger Achiever.

A loop had developed that made this a difficult situation to break. Constituents can become relatively autonomous. The Achiever, set up to gain approval, could not *accept* approval, because it always felt that it could have done better. It therefore prevented its own satisfaction. This was because had it allowed the sense of approval, the Achiever's dominant position would have been threatened. Steve might not have to strive so hard next time, and he might realize that he is acceptable for who he is. As an autonomous part of Steve, the Achiever was therefore serving its best interests by telling Steve that he could do better. So no approval reached the Longing Child, which remained a repressed part of Steve but did not disappear.

This put Steve into a double bind. He could not stop striving to achieve and he could not satisfy his longing. The only way out of this was to become able to step back from the situation and break the negative feedback loop. Unless he became aware of what was happening, he could not do that.

As Steve became aware of what was happening inside him, he learned about his constituents and discovered his Achiever. He explored the effects it was having on his life, its positive aspects but also where it held him back, and he learned that he could choose not to identify with it. He was able to allow the painful feelings of the Longing Child to surface in a safe environment. He came to see that both the Achiever and the Longing Child were parts of him, not the whole of him. Exploring his constituents was Steve's first step towards being able to free himself from the unconscious power of his constituents.

## OUR MULTIPLICITY

The concept of different parts of ourselves has long been accepted in the world of psychology. In his excellent book on psychosynthesis, *What We May Be*, Piero Ferruci states:

> One of the most harmful illusions that can beguile us is probably the belief that we are an indivisible,

immutable, totally consistent being … We can easily perceive our actual multiplicity by realizing how often we change our general outlook … Our varying models of the universe color our perception and influence our way of being. And for each of them we develop a corresponding self-image and a set of body postures and gestures, feelings, behaviors, words, habits and beliefs. The entire constellation of elements constitutes in itself a kind of miniature personality.[2]

This miniature personality may be more prevalent in one part of our lives, but appears in many aspects. So someone with a bossy constituent may find that this most often appears in his role as a sergeant-major, but it may also come out in how he treats his friends and family.

Abraham Maslow highlighted the importance of exploring the different aspects of our personalities. He wrote:

The study of the 'innards' of the personality is one necessary base for the understanding of what a person can communicate in the world, and what the world is able to communicate to him. We should expect communication with the outer world to improve along with improvement in the development of the personality, along with its integration and wholeness, and along with freedom from civil war between the various portions of the personality. These portions of us which are rejected and relegated to unconscious existence can and inevitably do break through into open effects upon our communication, affecting our perceptions as well as our actions.[3]

*Connecting inner and outer*

Maslow makes the connection between the direct impact of improvements in the inner world of the personality on both what we are able to communicate and what we can have communicated to us. Someone operating from a pessimistic constituent finds it hard to hear good news and see the potential in a project, always expecting things to go wrong. Maslow also acknowledges the conflict that can exist between the different parts of the personality, and the potential strength of that conflict, by describing it as a 'civil war'. He also stresses the effect that unconscious factors have on our ability to communicate, in other words on our ability to interact with the external environment.

A central part of inner leadership is learning to recognize and explore parts of our personalities so we are not taken over by unconscious factors. In this way, we can increase our choices and our clarity.

## GETTING TO KNOW YOUR CONSTITUENTS

We discover constituents by looking for traits and inflexible behavior across different aspects of our lives, such as the roles we play, our relationships with others, our personal history, our wants and desires, and the ideas we have about ourselves and our cultural environment. Going back to our bossy sergeant-major, if he were only bossy when in the role of sergeant-major, that would not be a constituent, because being a sergeant-major requires you to be bossy. But if he is bossy in other parts of his life and finds it hard not to be, then that could be a constituent.

I mentioned some common constituents in the previous chapter. Others include the protector, the controller, the critic, the persecutor, the demanding child and the top dog/underdog. There are no restrictions and everyone can make their own list.

## Exercise 6 – Discovering your constituents

Before you begin this exercise, give your motivation a boost by remembering your purpose for learning inner leadership. What is it that you want to achieve by spending time doing this? How might working with constituents help you? Check your willingness to proceed with this.

Spend about 30 minutes on this exercise. This means that you will be working fairly quickly, which has its advantages. You will have time to do a first pass of the exercise and use material that occurs to you, rather than doing too much thinking and editing. Take notes as you proceed. Do the exercise light-heartedly. Enjoy it. Be curious about what you are finding. The unconscious mind works better like this.

We are looking here at various aspects of life to find the traits, the inflexible behavior and the characteristics that signify constituents.

## Roles

Begin by thinking about the different roles you play. Can you identify distinct roles where you feel you are almost a different person? You could, for example, be acting as a leader, a peer, a spouse, a parent, a sports player, a driver. Are there fixed behavior and thought patterns that you take on in these roles? What feelings are involved in specific roles? What do you want in each role? Are there any subroles? Name these roles, e.g the leader, the challenging leader.

## How we are with people

Think about the different faces you present to the world under different circumstances. How do you behave with your spouse, mother, or friend compared to when you are in a work situation? How do you behave at work with a boss, a peer, a person of the opposite sex or someone much lower down the organization?

See if you can take a specific situation and move from the specific to a more general view of your behavior. For example, if you are highly organized at work and you carry this trait into other aspects of your life – perhaps where it is not so apt, like insisting that your children always stand next to each other according to height or age – you may find that you have an organizer as a constituent!

Our relationships are also like mirrors we hold up in front of ourselves, if we are willing to look. For example, if you always feel uncomfortable with a certain person, what might be the source of that discomfort? Depending on your relationship with them, it might be about authority, or perhaps they remind of you someone important in your life, or you see a part of yourself in them. We often see in others things we are unwilling to accept in ourselves. This is called projection. If you find yourself criticizing someone for something, look for that in yourself. It may bring you towards a constituent.

Take a few of these observations and explore the feelings associated with them. Is there a particular need or want you can identify?

It will also help you if you look back at Exercise 4 on recognizing qualities (page 33). Consider the qualities you feel are most dominant in you. Are some of these present in many different aspects of your life? This will give you a broad indication of some of the constituents you have. For example, you may be controlling, or respectful. Perhaps you are only controlling in certain situations, or with certain types of people.

*Qualities*

Think of the skills you possess and what these might tell you about your constituents.

*Skills*

What inner voices do you have – such as a critical voice, a fearful voice, a confident voice – that come to the fore in certain situations?

*Inner voices*

Remember to keep working quickly. If you get stuck, move on. Now think of things you want. These might include wealth, health, fame, love, success, power, peace, enlightenment – whatever is important to you. They tell you a great deal about yourself and your identifications.

By now you will have discovered a number of possible constituents. You should be able to see some of the diversity existing within you. Include both the things you do not like and feel less comfortable with and those you like. Look for ones that seem common, or familiar, or attract you, or with which you identify strongly. Pick some out of your list.

## Exercise 7 – Exploring your constituents

Put aside a further 15 minutes for each constituent. Choose two with which you identify reasonably strongly, and start to consider these as personalities within you. Think about what might be behind this constituent. Do this lightly, with some humor.

*Describing constituents*

- Give each constituent a descriptive name (e.g. Dan Dare, Pushy Penny, The Terminator, Miss Efficient).
- What physical characteristics would they have?
- Roughly how old would they be?
- What sort of clothes would they wear?
- How would they sound?
- What would their attitudes and behaviors be like?
- What would they like and dislike?
- What would they complain about?
- Draw a cartoon character of each one or make a mask.
- Which of them seems vested with the most power?
- Do you like them?

For each constituent, notice your physical, emotional and thought reactions when working on them. Go through Exercise 3 (page 31). Make a note of your reactions and what these tell you about how you feel about each constituent.

Try to find time later to look closely at more of your stronger constituents.

**YOU ARE NOT A CONSTITUENT**

Now take a piece of paper and draw an outer circle and an inner circle. Write down the names of your constituents in the outer circle. The inner circle represents your center of identity, the part of you that is not a constituent at all (see Chapter 10). Constituents are part of you, but you are not them, in the same way that you have a leg, but you are not your leg. There are probably some you like and some you don't like. This is fine. It is a step in being honest with yourself, so feel good about it.

We don't have to get rid of the constituents we don't like. Those we don't like may still have aspects that are beneficial to us given the right circumstances. See if you can accept these for what they are, in the same way that you may try to tolerate and understand a person you don't particularly like. After all, if such a person comes into our lives, as a work colleague or a customer, we may try to avoid them, but for the most part we have to learn how to get on with them and work with them, perhaps finding ways to minimize the things that annoy us.

This is very much the way I want you to think about your constituents. We have to find a way to work with them. We cannot just exterminate them. This is a psychological law: the more you try to get rid of an aspect of yourself, the stronger it becomes. We have to find more subtle ways to manage them.

---

**CASE NOTES 6**
**THE INFLUENCE OF A CONSTITUENT**

Martin, an international tax partner with a top firm of accountants, has a resentful adolescent as one of his constituents. His adolescent life had been difficult and he was still trying to work through some issues. This resentful adolescent constituent was generally unhelpful in leadership and work roles.

His constituent's catchphrase is 'I can't be bothered'. This constituent tends to take over when Martin feels particularly pressurized and overloaded with work. Unfortunately, this is precisely the time when he needs to communicate with other people and think clearly. Instead, he tends to criticize and devalue the company, his colleagues and the work. He communicates poorly and abruptly with others and his motivation falls. He also tends towards arrogance and fast judgments, which make other people feel criticized and defensive – not at all what is needed for a team to complete a task and meet a deadline.

Martin had felt that this must be an intrinsic part of him, so he wouldn't be able to change. When he recognized it as a constituent and he could see how it came about, he learned to choose to step out of it. He now recognizes its signs before it really takes a hold.

---

CONSTITUENTS CAN TAKE
YOU OVER

Constituents have a real effect on behavior. They are powerful. Sometimes there is an indication that they have been in control, when people say things like 'I don't know what came over me' or 'I wasn't feeling myself'.

You don't need to judge yourself for having certain constituents. Remember, for every quality you have, you also have some of the opposite. We only know light because we have dark, joy because we have sorrow, efficiency because we have inefficiency. The question of how the constituent helps you is very important. The various constituents are a part of you. They carry a quality that has become degraded from its purer form. In Steve's case, the quality of excellence had been degraded into achievement at all costs, no longer an active choice.

Awareness of a constituent is the first step to being free of its influence. You cannot change a behavior or a thought pattern until you are aware of it. The second part is to see how strongly you are identified with that particular constituent.

---

## Exercise 8 – Seeing a constituent's effect

- Choose one of the constituents you have already profiled.
- In what situations does it tend to be dominant?
- Does it tend to come out with particular people? What roles do those people have in your life? What do they represent to you?
- How much of the time is this constituent dominant?
- How does this constituent help you?
- How might this constituent hinder you in meeting your objectives or being how you want to be?
- What might be the need behind the constituent (e.g. success, regard, fear)?
- What is the principal quality being expressed by the constituent?
- Are there times when you would like to act from a different constituent?
- Think of a situation when your constituent has not been appropriate or helpful. What behavior might be more appropriate in this situation or with this person?

If you find a constituent that is dominant, in which you spend a great deal of time in a number of different situations, then this is a strong identification for you. It is important to look at the need behind the identification. For example, if you are identified with an achiever constituent, perhaps the need is for recognition or success or a fear of being wrong. If you can see what the need really is, you can judge its importance to you now, and if there might be more appropriate ways to satisfy it.

## Exercise 9 – Working with your constituents

Decide which of your constituents are particularly active in your work role, perhaps in:

● dealing with your team and/or peers;
● decision making;
● facing tough situations;
● some specific roles you play;
● taking the lead.

List constituents active in each area and write down the effect they have on your behavior and attitudes. Think of a specific example from the recent past for each area.

Learn to be aware of these constituents in working situations. See if you can identify if a constituent is dominant next time you are in a situation that you find stressful or challenging. At this stage, don't necessarily try to change anything. Just notice it.

When you have time afterwards, write down what you saw. Make a note of the feelings, attitudes and behaviors associated with the constituent. How do those align with the feelings, attitudes and behaviors you would like to have in that situation? Is the need behind the constituent still important to you? Perhaps there is another way in which it can be satisfied.

Make a note of any constituents that you would like to use less and ones that you would like to use more.

Remember, awareness is the key to being able to change.

Freeing ourselves from constituents with which we identify is the subject of Chapter 11.

# 6 Exploring Your Mindsets

## WHAT ARE MINDSETS?

Mindsets are the deep beliefs, attitudes, prejudices, views, self-concept and norms that we hold about ourselves and the world. They fundamentally affect our decisions and our behaviors.

Because they are the filter through which we see the world, they color our judgments, our thoughts, our feelings and our actions. Through our mindsets we create our own reality. The same data is viewed very differently by people with different mindsets. We tend to hold on to what we know, so mindsets only change when they are in marked opposition to reality, and even then they often change reluctantly. We see what we expect and want to see, confirming our view of things. This is why the past has such great power over the future.

## THE INFLUENCE OF MINDSETS

Mindsets have a direct impact on behavior. If you hold a mindset that the world is against you, it will seem to be that way. Remember Greg in Case notes 3. His mindset, that he was incompetent and would be exposed as a fraud, profoundly affected the way he worked and lived. The payoff is that your world view is confirmed as being right, and therefore, at that level, all is well.

One way to experience a mindset is to think of a subject and explore your beliefs and assumptions relating to it. Take money. What do you think of money? Do you want it? How much would you feel comfortable earning, and for what? Is it good or bad? What do you think of people who have a lot of money, or none?

In his book *Global Mind Change*, Willis Harman states:

> Each of us holds some sets of beliefs with which we conceptualize our experience – beliefs about history, beliefs about things, beliefs about the future, about what is to be valued, or about what one ought to do.[1]

## THE IMPORTANCE OF MINDSETS

Mindsets are often so deep that we are not conscious of them or of how they affect us. It is nevertheless important to be aware of the mindsets we hold if we are to be free to see the real needs of each situation. The objective of knowing and understanding our mindsets is to be able to change our behavior and the criteria on which we make decisions.

Exploring your mindsets enables you to know your basic assumptions and beliefs about life and work and see if they are still appropriate to you. We tend to hold on to thoughts and assumptions long after they cease to be appropriate. Thinking can become habitual. It saves having to rethink everything continually. Finding a balance will prove very useful in helping you to approach each situation with what it needs.

Again, you will find this easier to do if you don't judge yourself in relation to the mindsets you hold. There is no need. There has been a good reason for you to hold each of these mindsets, at one time in your life. We are looking here at what *is*. We are seeking those mindsets with which you identify most strongly and which no longer serve you.

**QUESTIONING YOUR BASIC ASSUMPTIONS**

One positive effect of a mindset can be found in the story of SouthWest Airlines.[2] CEO Herb Kelleher was sustained through difficult times by his belief that American society is based on values such as decency and fairness. In his 'David and Goliath' battle for survival against the major airlines, which he considered would do everything in their power to put SouthWest out of business, his determination was bolstered by a larger issue. If they succeeded in defeating him, he would have to admit to himself that his deep trust in his own people and society had been unfounded. If these would allow SouthWest to be driven out of business, he would have to reexamine his basic assumptions.

*Layers of mindsets*

We have layers of mindsets. There are those near the surface that are easily accessible, such as the belief that 'leaders need to be charismatic', or that 'people are motivated by money'.  There are intermediate ones that are more resistant to challenge. These might include long-held assumptions that are so ingrained we barely know we hold them any longer. Examples could be our attitudes and beliefs with regard to institutions, race and gender. We need deeper awareness and skills to look at them. Then there are core beliefs, deeply unconscious assumptions about ourselves and reality. These control our levels of self-esteem and are the basis of our self-concept and our whole disposition, for example optimism or pessimism. These core beliefs are very hard to change, and in many people will remain the same throughout their lifetimes. When they do change, the allied changes in behavior are profound.

*Unconscious mindsets control us*

As with our constituents, the more unconscious something is, the more it has the power to influence us because the harder it is to see. Therefore we need to explore mindsets in a disciplined way. Again, we are not trying to banish mindsets and replace them with new ones. We are trying to see the dominant ones and those we don't know much about so that we can become more flexible in our approach to them. We need to identify those that will help us lead our lives in the way we want.

## CASE NOTES 7
## THE INFLUENCE OF A MINDSET

Adam founded and runs a law practice, employing half a dozen lawyers. He holds a deep mindset that he picked up in childhood, which is 'No pain – no gain'. This was almost a family motto. His grandfather had pulled himself out of poverty by his bootstraps and passed a strong work ethic on to Adam's father. The family considers itself working class and Adam was the first to go to university. He does not expect success to come easily. He only feels that he is doing something worthwhile if it causes him stress.

Consequently, he does not look for the easy way of achieving things. Neither does he expect the people who work for him to find life easy. He has developed a culture in his business of high stress, long hours and perfectionism. Only similar people find it possible to work with him for long periods.

Adam is strongly identified with this mindset. He sees it as an inherent part of his personality. He applies it in other parts of his life. He does not take easily to leisure activities, viewing them as a waste of time. His children have to work the hardest at school. He has become a serious and heavily burdened person who would benefit greatly from 'lightening up'. He has built a successful business, but it has been a grind; he does not charge enough for his services, and it has been at great cost to himself and others working with him. It has not been a place of fun and consequently many talented people have stayed a short time and left, which has held the business back.

Adam is not conscious of the mindset that is ruling much of his life. It is a deep one, because it is part of his family culture and plugs into a work ethic held by millions of people. The mindset is also strong because, to someone who holds it, it has virtue on its side. Adam prides himself in practicing excellent law for people with little money to spend, but he also undercharges people who can afford his services. The downside of this is his undervaluing himself and the other people who work with him, and the fact that he is not doing it out of conscious choice.

To change this situation Adam will have to be willing to challenge his way of looking at the world and be prepared to suffer the consequent discomfort. Exercises 10, 11 and 12 in this chapter would be helpful should he choose to do this.

Mindsets that are buried deep in our unconscious find ways to express themselves, even if they are in contradiction to the conscious world. Often we try to smooth out the contradictions, because we want to be unified, consistent and reliable people, for our own sakes as much as for others. That, in itself, is a common mindset. But the belief system someone holds does not have to be consistent; in fact, it almost never is. There may be contradictory beliefs that typically do not come into conscious awareness at the same time. We may even try unconsciously to suppress evidence that reveals the contradiction. In this way, we can become very selective about what we see, what we remember and the way we interpret events.

Mindsets are not positive or negative. They are what is. A seemingly negative mindset, such as pessimism, is positive if it shields you from danger. Optimism can be harmful if it is not realistic. So mindsets in themselves are neutral. It is the strength and appropriateness of our identification with them that cause a lack of freedom of choice.

## MINDSETS PRESERVE THE STATUS QUO

Mindsets play a significant role in preserving the status quo. We hang on to our beliefs about things, making it difficult to find something really new. For example, designs change slowly, not because what we have is the best there could possibly be, but because it is difficult to see something with new eyes. How often, when something does change radically, do we think to ourselves, 'What a great idea, why didn't I think of that?'

Those who are able to think differently create huge commercial opportunities. They take the lead and create value and wealth. A good recent example of this is the people and companies who have gone beyond traditional thinking and used the internet as an effective way of doing business, for example retailer Amazon and stockbroker Charles Schwab. In only a few years each has achieved a market penetration and a stock market value that were previously unthinkable. Awareness of these mindsets could dramatically increase the success of companies which hold them.

## GLOBAL MINDSETS

There were some enormous shifts in mindsets during the previous millennium, which had greater effects on the world than physical and technological changes. The Copernican revolution, breaking the belief that Earth is the center of the universe and the epitome of creation, caused profound shock. It fundamentally changed the power base held by religion. It heralded the triumph of scientific inquiry over dogma.

Seeing Earth from space for the first time enabled us to see the beauty of our planet, but also its vulnerability in the vast reaches of space. We could view it for the first time as a whole. We were seeing it with new eyes. This was instrumental in our shift to recognizing that we are a part of a greater whole. It moved us towards the global mindset that we are all citizens of Earth and therefore have some responsibility for it.

## ORGANIZATIONAL MINDSETS

Mindsets are also present at the organizational level. People in organizations frequently follow norms that have long since outlived their usefulness. It is difficult to change the way things have always been done. The system supports it. If you do things the same way, you are unlikely to be blamed. To change is to put yourself at risk. In my work with companies, the question 'Why do you do things like this?' is often greeted with an embarrassed silence, followed by: 'I don't really know. We have always done it like this.'

Remember the quote from Raj Dhingra of 3Com in Chapter 1. In order to reinvent the company the vice-president in charge of the division knew that he had to change the prevailing mindset of the leader as hero with all the answers. Without that, he did not think he could access the creativity necessary for the organization to remain the market leader in the future.

---

### CASE NOTES 8 – A CORPORATE MINDSET

I have been working with a company that runs on the mechanistic, cause-and-effect, Newtonian mindset. It has two problems to tackle. One is cutting production costs, the other is raising the quality of output. These two problems are viewed separately and simplistically.

Cutting costs is seen as an easy process of gaining better deals from suppliers, reducing the number of people on each shift by building in better processes, and reviewing machine use. Each of these is considered in relative isolation. But there is a more complex view. Cutting costs is related to the quality problem. Reducing the cost of supplies may affect the quality of supply materials and delivery. Reducing the number of people on a shift may mean that problems are not spotted as quickly, increasing machine downtime and putting a greater burden on quality control. Redoing work is demotivating and expensive. Redundancies affect morale and productivity. Increasing machine use, at the same time as decreasing downtime for servicing, may be impossible. There could also be consequences that cannot be predicted.

The quality problem is also looked at

mechanistically. It is seen to be the remit of the operations director. It is up to him to solve it. The problem is seen simply as a lack of attention to detail and a fault of the production process and the quality control system.

Consternation was caused when a newly appointed director, who had been with the company for a number of years but had never previously thought it part of his brief to speak out, suggested that the quality problem had been building up for years. He was more attracted to the new physics and chaos theory than simple cause and effect. He saw the situation as a consequence of various actions that were related not only to production, but also to capital finance decisions, customer expectations, the culture of the company, the morale and attitudes of staff who have seen colleagues made redundant each year for nearly 10 years, supply policies, processes used, quality control being only at the end of the production system, and a host of other, in themselves seemingly small factors.

The consternation was brought about because solving these problems would mean that the senior management team had to work together in a completely new way. They could no longer carry out their different roles in isolation. It would involve them in having to communicate more openly with each other, stop hiding mistakes, support each other, pursue common goals and think in a different way. I have been working with each of them separately to help them explore their own particular mindsets in relation to this and the ensuing changes in attitudes and behavior necessary for progress to be made.

The mindsets of company leaders are, according to Arie de Geus in his book *The Living Company*,[3] a major reason that the lives of so many companies are short. The average life expectancy is just 40 years for a multinational company in the Fortune 500 or its equivalent. De Geus reckons that

*Mindsets can be costly*

many chief executives today are stuck in a mindset, a conventional wisdom, that 'conserving and maximizing capital' is a company's most important goal.

Fifty years ago that goal was indeed important. Capital was relatively scarce and companies needed to compete for it. Investors were conservative. But the mindset no longer reflects today's imperatives, when the world of business has shifted from one dominated by capital to one dominated by knowledge. Capital is no longer the scarcest thing. One of the reasons behind the rises of stock markets in recent years is the 'wall of money' that pension and insurance funds have available for investment. There is a glut of capital. The deficiency lies in the limited role that ideas and creativity are allowed to play in the creation of wealth. It is individuals, the 'community of humans', who make the difference.

Mindsets are often slow to adapt to reality. The successful companies are those that are able to adapt them quickly, which requires that individuals adapt theirs equally fast.

Below are some of the more common mindsets I have encountered in my work with business managers, all of which have a profound effect on the effectiveness of the organizations in which they work.

**Only people at the top have good ideas.** This is based on hierarchical structure, command and control, and information is power. It creates a culture of disempowerment and dependence. Companies that have given this mindset up have achieved remarkable results when they have listened to ideas from all parts of the organization. After all, it is the people with direct customer interface and daily experience of the processes who can see improvements most clearly. One company I worked with allowed its employees to invest £100,000 in reorganizing the paint shop, and saved over £300,000 a year. *Alternative*: we need all the good ideas we can get, from whatever source, if we are to be successful.

**People cannot change the way they are**. This is often cited as a good reason for not trying something new. It is sometimes senior managers, who have been with the company a long time and whose success has been built on the old ways, who find change most difficult. People can often change the way they behave at work if they know why they are making the changes and if they are motivated and supported to do so. GCV is a good example of this (see Case notes 1 in Chapter 1). Those scientists did change the way they saw themselves and the world. They had to in order to achieve their aims. As another illustration, by involving staff in the changes, a paper-making company implemented a new production process in a quarter of the time it thought this would take. *Alternative*: people are flexible and we can change our behaviors and attitudes.

**If it's worked in the past, it will work in the future**. This is a version of 'If it ain't broke, don't fix it'. But the markets, the technology, the customers and the employees are changing all the time. This avoids new thinking and preserves the status quo. Companies that are unable to adapt do not survive long. Some companies, such as Stora and DuPont, have survived a very long time because they have been prepared to completely redefine themselves. *Alternative*: let's look at current reality and try out some changes based on our observations.

**People are only motivated by money**. People *are* motivated by money, but it is the lowest common denominator and therefore the easiest answer to the problem. I know a very disenchanted 30 year old with a six-figure salary and a luxury car. But he has no authority, is treated as a fee-earning machine, works such long hours he has had to forgo his social life and is thinking of giving it all up. Money has become less important than a fulfilling life, respect as an individual, personal authority and the opportunity to influence the way his company operates away from what he calls 'the android culture'.

*Alternative*: people's needs are complex and can be understood if an open atmosphere is created and you take the time to listen to them.

**Suppliers/customers are out to get you**. Winning in business requires confrontation. Smart companies are now building collaborative relationships with customers and suppliers, where product development and supply chains are built together. They are looking beyond short-term pricing pressures for longer-term benefits from their relationships. An example of this was the building of the infrastructure of the Heathrow Express railway. The project was thrown into disarray when a tunnel collapsed. In the construction industry, what was likely to follow was a cycle of blame, recrimination and lawsuits. But the project's senior managers decided to go a different route, and encourage the various parties to collaborate and work together to get the project back on course. This involved an enormous shift in mindsets for many people, achieved by individual and team coaching. The result was a project that delivered on time. *Alternative*: we will win through collaboration.

**You should not challenge authority (e.g. us)**. If you think that, then you have to come up with all the ideas as well. A client of mine works in a professional practice as a manager. Decisions are made by the partners before management meetings. Managers who have challenged basic assumptions in the past have not made it to partnership. This is not conducive to innovation, so people who have creativity and good ideas eventually leave. *Alternative*: it is the role of leaders to create an atmosphere where everything can be challenged, including themselves.

**There is no room for emotions or personal issues in business**. If you ask people to be constricted into a certain mode when they are at work, inevitably they learn not to bring parts of themselves to their job, which often includes their creativity and their passion. This attitude creates monocultures, where difference is not seen to be an advantage, cutting off the flow of ideas and creating a sterile environment. *Alternative*: we will encourage people to bring more of themselves to work.

**Problems should be solved as soon as possible**. Of course, some problems need to be fixed quickly, but if this is the general attitude it can be hard to live with a problem for a while so that you can see it anew and find an answer that may bring about long-term improvement. This way of doing things often covers up a culture where mistakes are not tolerated, where blaming happens and people are fearful of being seen to be wrong. *Alternative*: allow problems to remain unsolved for long enough for new solutions to be created.

GETTING TO KNOW YOUR MINDSETS

## Exercise 10 – Discovering your mindsets

If you are willing, do this exercise to discover some of your mindsets. Remember your purpose for doing this work. Ask yourself the following questions, spending just a couple of minutes on each. Write down your answers. Again, work quickly and lightly, giving the unconscious a chance to operate. If you get stuck, move on.

- What do you tend to criticize yourself for?
- What embarrasses you?
- What causes do you support?
- What makes you angry?
- What subjects make you feel defensive?
- Which thoughts are hardest to talk to your spouse or colleagues or friends about?
- What opinions do you often express?
- What assumptions do you hold about groups of people, races, religions, genders?
- Do you have some assumptions about particular people, such

as your boss, people in your team, your mother, the Prime Minister etc.?
● Which way do you think the world is heading?
● What do you think about yourself?
● What do you want most in life?

You may have additional questions you want to ask yourself. From this initial trawl, see if you can identify a few deeply held beliefs, prejudices or attitudes. If you have found this difficult, try thinking about your attitudes and beliefs around some of the subjects listed below. Alternatively, you could talk this through with someone who knows you well and whose opinion you trust, or with your mentor or co-mentor.

Mindset subjects:

| | |
|---|---|
| big business | capital punishment |
| taxation | learning a new language |
| the government | religion |
| fat/thin people | homosexuality |
| money | your boss |
| the police | the environment |
| rich/poor people | the lottery |
| your parents | marriage/divorce |
| your children | transport policy |
| the next generation | yourself as a leader/parent/ |
| computer technology | friend/spouse/driver/ |
| genetic engineering | intellectual etc. |
| nature vs nurture | |

## Exercise 11 – Seeing the effects of mindsets

Now choose some mindsets from your list and do the following exercise (taking no more than 10 minutes for each one):

1  Think of a deeply held belief, assumption, expectation or attitude that you hold. Write it down on a piece of paper. This is a mindset.
2  How does this mindset influence your behavior?

3 How strong is this mindset? How long have you held it? How often does it come up?
4 How does holding this mindset benefit you? Look for some kind of payoff, even if it is not obvious at first.
5 How might this mindset hinder you? What does it stop you from seeing or doing?
6 Can you see what might be behind the mindset? What need is it serving? Does it relate particularly to one of your constituents?
7 Is there a quality you can see underlying the mindset?

---

As you can see, the process of discovering mindsets is very similar to working with our constituents, as we did in Exercise 6 (page 59). Mindsets also have been formed to protect us at a particular time, because we felt we had to conform, or we had to be different; because we needed to believe something to make sense of our world; because we had to feel safe and take away confusion; or because we had to believe something about ourselves. The reasons are many, but there always is one. And, as in the case of constituents, each mindset has a quality attached to it that has been degraded or distorted from its purer form. When you reflect deeply on your mindsets, you will find that quality, which is now at your disposal.

---

**CASE NOTES 9**
**EXAMPLE OF A MINDSET**

1 **Mindset: I know best**. This was often my attitude at work when I was younger. It had an arrogant element to it. It could also be: 'If you want something doing properly, do it yourself.'
2 The effect of this mindset on my behavior was that I tended to be very self-sufficient in my work. I did not consult with others very often. It meant that I approached my work with confidence and I could work quickly and efficiently to complete tasks.

3   I had held this mindset for a long time. My parents had taught me to be independent. I went to a boarding school, where you have to get on with things yourself. I found school work easy and did not have much respect for many of the staff. I chose jobs that gave me much autonomy to create my own client base and my own working methods. I was confident that I should do well because I had been told I had a high level of intelligence.

4   This mindset served me because it allowed me to get on with things confidently and without interference. That way I could complete my work as I wanted to. It also meant that my ideas were not challenged. I did not take criticism well at that time, seeing it as a threat. I did not have to relate to many other people, which made me feel safe. I could easily cover any mistakes. If I was struggling with something, people did not know, which was good. In that way, I was not exposed.

5   How did this hinder me? It would have been good to share ideas with other people. It would have broadened my view and acted as a stimulus. I did not change the way I did things very much. I sometimes felt isolated and would have liked more interaction with others. I would have felt as though I belonged to the company for which I was working. The problem with insulating myself from feedback was that I did not often get positive feedback either. So I really had no way of knowing whether I was doing well or not until my annual assessment, unless something went very right or very wrong. This mindset also stopped me from taking more responsibility at work, building a team around me. Managing other people might have been satisfying. Perhaps I would not have had to work such long hours then, just to get things done.

6   What is behind this mindset? I was surprised that I came up with comments about not wanting to deal

with people and receive their feedback. Feedback in the past was often negative, the 'you could do even better' syndrome. I found it easier to be self-contained and I found it difficult to trust people. My view of the world was that I would not meet expectations or live up to my potential. My arrogance was set up to cover this feeling of insecurity.

7   I wanted to be considered 'good enough'. If I tried hard, I might fail, but at the same time my need was to fulfill my potential. It is no coincidence that, quite unconsciously, it is so important to me that people do have the opportunity to live to their full potential and that I should eventually choose this as my area of work. The quality behind this mindset is autonomy, to be able to trust myself as being OK and act according to my values and purpose.

Once I had seen this mindset and explored it, I was in a much better position to choose when it was useful to me and when it was a restriction. I felt it was doing me more harm than good and I decided to work to release myself from it most of the time, which meant dealing with some deep issues.

Note that there was no need to get rid of it completely. My intention was to use it less. If I had rid myself of it completely, then I would have been repressing it, driving it into my unconscious, and its strength would have grown.

It was also important to keep the good parts of it that were useful to me. The quality of autonomy enables me to make decisions, to work on my own, to initiate projects and be self-motivated. These are vital for writing a book, where you need to keep an independent mind, and for some consultancy work. But if I remain in this attitude all the time, I miss the valuable feedback that people give me and I would not be learning from the work I do.

## Exercise 12 – Exploring your mindsets

Try Exercise 11 on a number of the mindsets that influence you in your work. You could choose one for each of:

- Leading people.
- Making decisions.
- Having creative ideas.
- Your attitudes to change.
- Handling conflict or difference.
- Implementing your ideas.

Write notes on each part of the exercise. See how it is affecting you at work in these areas. Try to see both negative and positive aspects.

Over the next week or so, find a situation where you can work with each mindset. Do the exercise and record what effects this had on your physical, emotional and thinking reactions. Do not try to change the mindset, just notice it.

Through this you can build up a picture of what mindsets tend to be in place in certain types of situations. As you do this, notice your physical, emotional and mental reactions. Allow these reactions to tell you which mindsets are most important to you, which are the most dominant, which you feel least easy with and any other relevant information you can glean. Observe the language you use when you think and write about them. Your language may also give you important information.

Can you see how you have mindsets that are relatively fixed and how some of them are no longer relevant to your life? Do some serve you well? Can you see how they affect your behavior, how you relate to people, how you see the world, what decisions you make and how you lead people?

Sort the mindsets into groups according to their strength and their relevance to your life as it is now. Do not judge them. Each one has an element of truth in it and each has been held for a purpose that has served you well at sometime in your life.

Compare what you have found here with your view of yourself as a leader from Exercise 4 on qualities (page 33). Can you see a link between your mindsets and your attitudes to leadership?

Now draw two circles, one inside the other. Write your mindsets in the outer ring. The inner ring represents your center of identity, which does not hold any mindsets. Look at the mindsets and see that you are not them. You can choose to hold them, or choose not to hold them, depending on whether they are appropriate.

---

Uncovering mindsets is a freeing process, increasing clarity and choice. It is a vital part of the inner leadership work, so please spend some time on it.

Remain attentive to your strongest mindsets and how they influence your responses to people and situations. As you do this, you will find that the process becomes more natural and easier.

**MINDSETS KEEP US FROM REALITY**

# 7 *Discovering Your Values*

In the previous two chapters you explored some of the constituents and mindsets that influence you. The next two chapters will enable you to clarify your values and your purpose, so you can direct your energies in ways that are meaningful for you.

## WHAT ARE VALUES?

Values are deeply held beliefs, but of a particular type. Values come from a sense of discrimination of what is right or not right for us, of what is desirable. They constitute a code according to which we choose to live. Values can be used as a basis for decision making, allowing us to place possible ways of behaving into some approval–disapproval hierarchy, adding an element of predictability. A shared value system not only guides an individual, but others too.

Maslow[1] describes values in terms of the 'ought' questions: What ought I to do? What ought I to be? This is not what we ought to be for someone else, but in order to live according to our own integrity. Values tend to be beliefs that we think are worthwhile, that go beyond our living entirely for ourselves. In this way they are beyond the personal, because they are in service of something.

It is important that we discover what our own values are and don't just accept those given to us by our upbringing and our society. Only if values make sense to you, in your own experience, will they be meaningful and will you want to adhere to them.

## VALUES AS FRAMEWORKS

In a world that increasingly demands that we deal with open-ended systems and an uncertain future, where fixed long-term plans are less and less relevant, we need to find frameworks and boundaries within which we can make decisions and thereby translate our inner world into our outer one. Values can fulfill this role. They act as points of reference that influence decision making, behavior and attitudes. They are a vital part of inner leadership. How else do you determine what you choose in life out of all the hundreds and thousands of decisions you could make? Values can act as a guide and an anchor to help with this process.

For example, if faced with a problem to solve you may have a hierarchy of values to go through in order to find a solution with which you are happy. The first may be that the solution should be within the law of the country. It may be important to you to go beyond this and to adhere to an additional ethical code, such as that the solution should not cause direct harm to others, or that it should positively benefit others. It may be a value that you serve your company well, which is run for profit, so another value to take into account is that profits should not suffer.

You may have other values that you want to take into account. If you value aesthetics highly, the solution may need to be elegant, or simple, or artistic. If you value the autonomy of people highly, the decision may be influenced by the fact that you don't want to be prescriptive to others. The possibilities are endless, which is why it is so important to know your own values and the extent to which you want them to influence you.

## VALUES IN ORGANIZATIONS

If we are aware of our values and use them to guide our behavior, we can be confident that we are doing the right thing for ourselves. Values play a similar role within an organization. They have been described as the glue that sticks everything together. According to Robert de Haas, CEO of Levi Strauss: 'Values provide a common language for aligning a company's leadership and its people'.

*Values are more than good words*

Values need to be reflected in the company's processes, demonstrated by the leader's personal behavior, used in difficult situations, incorporated into management and reward systems and stated clearly. However, people will not be influenced by values unless they agree with them, so a company's values must not go radically against those held by its people.

Some companies are obviously strongly values led, such as cosmetics retailer The Body Shop and ice-cream company Ben and Jerry's. But all companies are run according to some values. We may not always agree with them, but there is no denying that they are there.

SouthWest Airlines sees values as the 'emotional rules that govern our behavior and attitudes', according to Kevin and Jackie Freiberg.[2] They list the company's values as follows:

- Profitability
- Ownership
- Low cost
- Family
- Legendary service
- Hard work
- Altruism
- Individuality
- Love
- Egalitarianism
- Common sense
- Simplicity

This is a wide range of values. Individuals will identify more with some of them than with others. Some are pragmatic and designed to make sure that the company runs profitably and survives for the future. Others are what many people would associate more readily with the term 'values', concepts such as egalitarianism and altruism. Some, such as love, are unusual to espouse in the workplace, but are not necessarily absent.

At GCV (see Case notes 1), it was only once certain values of openness and honesty had been set that people could really connect to the purpose of the company and the need for it to grow very rapidly. The values exhibited by the CEO were the inspirational factor that enabled people to see that the process of change was possible, even though they knew much personal discomfort, and some casualties, would be suffered along the way.

## OUR VALUES REFLECT WHO WE ARE

Our real values are the ones we act by. They are also a strong motivator. If we lead our lives in a way that makes us feel good about ourselves, or at the very least feel comfortable, then we are more motivated to do what we do. Our values are personal. By discovering your values you are taking a big step towards learning who you really are.

Maslow writes:

What we have learned is that ultimately, the best way for a person to discover what he ought to do is to find out who and what he is, because the path to ethical and value decisions is via the discovery of facts, truth, reality, the nature of the particular person.[3]

So according to Maslow, the work we have been doing already will lead us naturally towards our values. It certainly provides a necessary basis for the following exercise.

## Exercise 13 – Discovering your values

First, write a list of the values you know you hold as important now. Look at them. Which are most important to you? Do they all make sense to you in your own experience, or have some been imposed on you?

Now go through the following steps to explore your values

more deeply, perhaps confirming those you have already identified, perhaps enabling you to expand the list, perhaps causing you to reconsider your original list.

Think of an activity you enjoy, something important to you. Don't worry too much about what it is. If you prefer, start with something light-hearted; it will still lead you to your values. I once started with vacuuming and ended up with the values of trust, honesty and self-respect.

Write a brief description of your chosen activity at the top of a page.

Now list all the aspects of the activity that you enjoy. For example, if you enjoy running, examples of aspects may be feeling exercised, being outside, pushing yourself to the limit, being with others, racing, gently jogging, feeling the sunshine, appreciating the countryside, being alone, time to reflect and many others.

Once you have recognized as many aspects as you can, pick out the two that seem to be most important, and ask yourself the question: 'Why is this so important to me?'. Each time you find an answer, repeat the question until you can go no deeper. For example, I like running because it gives me time to reflect. That is important to me because reflective time enables me to see things more clearly. That is important to me because seeing clearly helps me to respond appropriately. That is important to me because I want to lead my life with integrity. And so on. There is a fuller example of this process below.

**Go beyond the logical**

This exercise may lead you in unexpected directions, and eventually it will lead you to a place from which you can go no further. The fact that it may lead you in unexpected directions can bring unpredictable results. Don't worry if the answers you are receiving are not entirely logical. We want to get beyond how you would normally see yourself. It can be a way for the unconscious, for deeply buried thoughts, to rise to the surface. So allow this to happen and don't stop too early. Be prepared to struggle to go deeper.

Now look at the final statements you have made. Can you pick out their essence? What do they say about you and your values?

Try this exercise a number of times on different activities or roles, both from work and from your personal life, and see if you have clusters of values that form the basis of your value system. Now look at the roles you play and the major decisions you have made in your life. Which value has the greatest influence on them?

---

## CASE NOTES 10 – DISCOVERING VALUES

Here is an example of part of Exercise 13.

*Think of something I enjoy doing*: I enjoy facilitating a team of people brought together to manage a project.
   I enjoy:

- bringing people together to work;
- interaction with a diverse group of people;
- helping to create an atmosphere where everyone can participate;
- getting decisions by consensus;
- watching people grow in stature;
- being a team coach or mentor;
- creating firm boundaries for the meetings (time, agenda, rules);
- helping the team to attain its goals.

*The most important thing for me is*: helping to create an atmosphere where everyone can participate.

*Why is this important to me?*
Because I believe that everyone has something to contribute and should be allowed and encouraged to do that.
*Why is this important to me?*
Because it requires everyone to recognize that all opinions and views are valid and that differences can be accepted and brought together.

*Why is this important to me?*
Because I see individual egotism and narrow-mindedness as being divisive and counter-productive within groups and organizations. Dialogue and collaboration bring the best solutions.
*Why is this important to me?*
Because so much creativity and energy can be wasted, leaving people feeling demoralized and frustrated, and self-esteem falls.
*Why is this important to me?*
Because I want people to achieve their goals and aspirations and to feel good about themselves.
*Why is this important to me?*
Because so many people function at work on a low level of misery. Work should be a life-enhancing and positive experience that benefits everyone.
*Why is this important to me?*
Because I want business to be productive and something we can be proud of. It is not just about controlling, cost cutting, confrontation and winning at the expense of someone else, it is about achieving excellence, giving people the opportunity to do their best and to grow in stature as individuals.
*Why is this important to me?*
Because to grow as a person, in skills, in achievement and psychologically, leads to a sense of fulfillment. People deserve this.
*Why is this important to me?*
Because I have experienced this myself, and it makes life worth living and joyful. It enables people to shine and allow others to do the same. It creates an atmosphere where people can make their best contribution, leading to higher motivation, creativity, capacity for change and success.
*Why is this important to me?*
It feels like my life's work. I trained for this without realizing it. I want to help bridge the gap between individual needs and business goals, because at the

moment it is an area of conflict that spreads internal angst and misery at the same time as handicapping organizations.

I could probably go on with this, but I have reached a point where I can see the values involved. The main one is that people should have the opportunity to fulfill their potential, so valuing each person for who he or she is. This is the guiding principle behind much of my work. There are other values that also emerge, such as recognizing all views as having validity and that work should be a growing, life-enhancing experience. I also find that I have a strong desire for business to be the best it can be. As you can see, this process does meander around, but that is part of the creativity and the fun of doing it.

Once you have completed the exercise, and you are clearer about the values you hold, look at some decisions or actions you have taken recently. Did your decision or action fit in with your value system? Was it driven by your value system? If you had been more aware of your underlying values, would you have taken a different decision or action? Perhaps you can see a decision you made with which you feel uncomfortable, bringing you internal conflict. This kind of conflict usually brings feelings of guilt, shame or unease.

**ALIGNING DECISIONS WITH VALUES**

## CASE NOTES 11
## USING VALUES TO MAKE CHOICES

Nick was caught in such a conflict. He works in a dog-eat-dog culture, macho and unforgiving. It is a culture that breeds fear. You either make it by the time you're 40 or you're out. Nick can also see the excellence of the work and the high rewards for those who stay with it and succeed. He has developed a view that in order to succeed he has to play the same game, tough and

*Acting with clear understanding*

ruthless. He knows that he is tough on the people working for him when he feels that he is being watched by his boss, and then later he has to alleviate his guilt by making up to them.

Nick does not feel comfortable. He agonizes about what he does. He is beginning to recognize that he is doing things that are in conflict with his values of fairness and honesty. The important point is for him to be able to make a conscious decision to go ahead and be ruthless if that is really important to him, knowing that he is doing it and that this is not all he is. He still has that choice. The conflict is still powerful, but now it is conscious he has a context for it, making it more possible to handle.

Nick's awareness is helping him to approach this situation with a clear understanding of its needs. He recognizes the culture he is in, which he had a vague notion of before. He can see how this is in conflict with his values. He would like to achieve a partnership in the firm, and he is becoming clear about what sacrifices he is and is not prepared to make to achieve that.

This opens up his options. He can respond to situations and to what he can see. He can see the damage the culture causes because it creates conflicts in the lives of the people who work there.

The long hours required to succeed in that culture became a huge bone of contention in Nick's main personal relationship, straining it until it broke. In this relationship he had formed a pattern of neglect, followed by expensive treats or holidays by way of compensation. He was resentful about the impact of his work, and he needed to accept that it was his choice.

When pressure comes, Nick can see clearly the choices he has to make. If his intention is not to work sixty or more hours a week, he has choices around controlling his workload, balanced with how others will perceive his commitment. Perhaps there are more tasks he could delegate.

He has a choice around whether he wants to build a highly motivated and efficient team that could achieve success with less personal sacrifice, and therefore bring his own values into the situation. He has a choice ultimately around whether he feels he can do something to change the culture or whether he would be happier and more fulfilled at another firm.

He no longer feels caught in the situation, in the system, resenting the sacrifices he is making. Now he is in the process of choosing the best solution not only for himself, but also for the firm. If he could realistically make a change to the system that would benefit the firm and others, then all well and good. If he is not going to be able to contribute, it is best for him to leave and join another firm more in line with his values. His self-awareness has taken him from being a passive victim to being in the driving seat. He can decide with a high level of awareness.

Nick now feels much more in control of his destiny. He is no longer swept along by the demands and culture of the firm he works for, experiencing a vague sense of resentment and dissatisfaction. He knows that by remaining where he is, he is making a conscious decision. He is making changes that are within his circle of influence to suit his values and purpose, such as controlling his working hours, building competence below him so that he can delegate and treating people with respect.

He has found that he has done some of his best work recently, picking up and handling some major new accounts. He feels more competent and confident, stronger in himself.

## VALUES PROVIDE A STRONG BASE

Once we have awareness of our values, we have a strong basis for everything we do. We are less affected by short-term considerations and more consistent in our attitudes and behaviors. This will not make you more inflexible, in fact just the opposite. Inflexibility comes from being uncertain of our ground and therefore having to stick with something definite. If we are more aware of our values we can be more sure of our ground, and therefore we may make more surprising decisions on which we feel able to stand firm.

If you are self-aware you know immediately when your personal values are compromised. Better able to handle your internal conflicts, you do not have to repress them. Look out for the project that is more difficult to tell friends and family about, or the internal doubt about whether you really want to do something.

There will be times when your values are challenged, but if you are confident about them and about their real importance to you, you will naturally follow them. Or you may decide to make a compromise under certain circumstances. There may be a conflict that needs to be resolved, but at least you will know when you are compromising and you will be able to do so in a way that you can live with.

**SHARED VALUES**

Values can be shared and developed cooperatively to give an organization the same kind of strength that they offer on a personal basis. You cannot force somebody into a value system; that only causes compliance. In the same way that you have to decide your values for yourself, according to your personal experience, people need to enroll in organizational values of their own volition. Only if they do this will they become committed to them.

If values are explicit, and people do decide to adopt them, the effect on participation and motivation can be powerful. Values give people a context in which to work and they imbue the work with meaning.

Values influence a company's policies, goals, actions and behaviors. The choices taken are now within a framework of acceptable and measurable behaviors based on the system of values. It is then possible to monitor whether the policies and goals set are consistent with the values as well as with the vision and the strategy. Are policies consistent with commitment to the values, the employees, the customers, whatever is decided as relevant for that company? Are the actions taken bound by a required code of behavior, which is also consistent with the values?

## Exercise 14 – Using values in your work

Take a current situation in your work. This could be around a particular decision you are in the process of making or a creative project. Look carefully at the situation:

- How clearly do you think you are seeing what the situation needs?
- Might any constituents or strong mindsets be active, coloring your viewpoint?
- Can you see through these, and clean the filter?
- Do you think you have as full a picture as you need?
- Do any of your possible choices conflict with any of your values? Look at these carefully.
- Is there any conflict with what you perceive to be your organization's values?
- Are your organization's values in alignment with your own?
- What influence do your values have on the decision to be made, on how you might approach it, on how you behave in this particular instance?

Where you are left with a dilemma, use your values to help guide you to the right decision and see how you can do the best for yourself and your organization. Is there still a dilemma?

Write up this situation and what you have learned from it. Note particularly the effect your values have in terms of you taking the lead in your work.

# 8 Knowing Your Purpose

## PURPOSE DIRECTS ACTION

If a value is a conception of the desirable, a purpose determines the direction and the action to be taken, giving effort a specific direction. For example, openness is a value that gives us a framework in which to act, but it does not determine the specific direction of our energy. With something as broad as openness, it is easy to see how energy may become dissipated if there is not a clear purpose. Several people could hold openness as their primary value and pursue very different aims. For one it may be about honest relationships, for another creative expression, for another transparency in government, for another openness to learning.

## YOUR LIFE'S PURPOSE

I believe that each one of us has our own particular purpose in life. It is our overall aim, vision or intention. Mine is the discovery and expression of my true self, and part of my purpose is to help others achieve this, so increasing our opportunities to fulfil our potential. This purpose creates a context for our lives. It gives our lives meaning, telling us what is important and what is at stake. If we focus our attention where our purpose lies, we automatically create a high level of motivation for ourselves. But many of us have never known or have forgotten our life's purpose. It is important to reconnect to it and to make it conscious in order to live it.

## Exercise 15 – Discovering your purpose

Allocate twenty minutes to half an hour for this exercise and find somewhere quiet where you will not be disturbed. Have a piece of paper and a pen handy.

Imagine that you have only five years to live. Write down in detail the form your life would take:

- What would you do with your life?
- What work would you do?
- Where would you live?
- With whom would you spend more of your time?
- What would you want to learn?
- What qualities would you want to display?
- What else would be important to you?
- How hard would you fight to live?

Now imagine you have only six months to live. Do the same exercise.

Think about what you have written. What does this tell you about your purpose? See what you can distill from this.

I apologize for the morbidness of these exercises, but they are a good way of approaching your purpose. Now I would like you to write your own obituary. For what would you like to be remembered? How would you like to be described?

From this you will discover your purpose and see if it fits in with your values. Your values act as a checking system to make sure you are on track.

Look back at your notes on the last part of Exercise 5 (page 37), where you imagined yourself presenting your qualities as a self-leader. Compare your vision for yourself now, as formed by your values and purpose, to the one you drew up then.

As you were doing these exercises, what messages were you receiving from your body, your emotions and your thoughts? Perhaps you found a clear purpose. If you did not, don't worry. Keep it in the back of your mind and see what emerges over time.

If you find it difficult to think of your purpose, start by thinking of your vision of yourself, your work or your family. Believe that you will be led towards your purpose. Notice what you are drawn to. Look out for anything unusual happening to you. See what causes physical, emotional and mental reactions. Take note of your dreams. Read books or articles to which you feel particularly drawn. If you have an inkling, but you are not sure about it, work with that and see if it becomes clearer or if something else emerges.

## IS YOUR LIFE SUPPORTING YOUR PURPOSE?

If you now have an idea of an overall purpose, what aspects of your life support it? These will be your subordinate purposes, steps along the way. If you can see aspects of your life now that seem to be opposing your purpose, look at these carefully. Things that appear to be conflicting could be there as a means of learning that is necessary to keep you on track.

For example, you may need to have some outbursts of behavior of which you feel ashamed in order to see how you would prefer to behave. You may need to feel weak and disempowered in a situation to see how you disempower other people sometimes, or to put you in touch with the powerful part of yourself. See what adjustments you would have to make in order to align these elements. If, after careful consideration, you find that there are things that do not serve your purpose at all, you may decide to discontinue them. But always make sure that you have not missed their relevance before doing so.

## Exercise 16
## Linking values and purpose

Go back to what you discovered about your values. Which were of primary importance to you? Now write down the things you do in your life that are based on those values, that support them or where those values seem important.

What do these activities and the specific direction your life has taken tell you about your overall purpose? Can you see a trend in the things you do or the way you are? Write down as many as possible of the things you do. See if you can identify any patterns.

## Exercise 17
## Bridging current reality and your ideal

Using Exercises 15 and 16 as material, imagine what your ideal life would be like if you were living out your purpose and your values. Write down a profile of yourself. How would you be? What would your relationships with other people be like? What sort of job would you have? What would people think of you?

Think about your current reality compared to that vision of yourself. Identify the gaps between the two.

List a number of things you could do to bridge the gap between your current state and how you would be if you were fulfilling your purpose. These are areas where you could take the lead. I wonder if these are some of the things you think about doing, but don't get around to.

Choose the most important area for you now, and decide on two achievable things you could start with. These may be displaying different behaviors, acting on something you have been putting off, involving other people more closely, sharing information, putting your focus on a different area, being clearer about vision.

Think about how you could take these achievable things into your work. What would taking the lead mean for you in this context? Decide exactly what actions you can take, put a timescale on them and see what situations are the most appropriate for bringing them in. When you have achieved changes, find two more achievable things you can do, and so on.

All that is important is to be moving in the right direction, towards living your purpose. The entire vision you have of yourself may be too near to perfection to achieve. That is fine, as long as you see this as a journey with a direction, where the traveling is more important than the arriving. Set yourself achievable steps towards your target. Don't judge yourself for not having met them yet.

*Stage 3*

# Actualizing

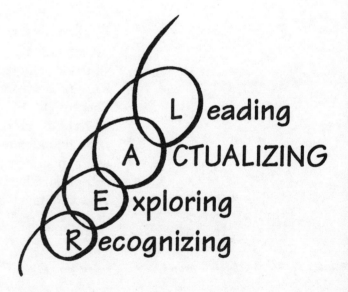

**L**eading

**A**CTUALIZING

**E**xploring

**R**ecognizing

## ACTUALIZING OUR CHOICES

Actualizing is the ability to act consciously and to choose our responses in alignment with our values and purpose. By seeing more clearly who we are and who we want to be, we give ourselves more choice in relation to how we respond to situations and events, enabling us to work at the leading edge of our creativity and effectiveness.

To respond to a situation and act in the here and now often means letting go of the past and allowing ourselves to change. In Chapter 9 we look at the process of how we change.

We find clarity when we are able to stand back, in the position of observer, and see ourselves in the context of our lives, in our environment and in our relationships. The place from which we can see clearly – our own internal observer – is our 'center of identity' (see Chapter 10).

We are able to choose our responses when we are able to free ourselves of our identifications with constituents and mindsets, to see anew the problem, situation or person facing us. We need to be willing to look at situations differently and take the risk of changing habitual behaviors. Freeing ourselves is the subject of Chapter 11.

To bring our choices into the external world we also need to understand and strengthen our innate will to grow as a human being (see Chapter 12) and to be able to accept ourselves as we are, knowing that we continue to grow and develop (see Chapter 13).

# How We Change 9

We all have an innate will to develop and grow. This is part
of our evolution as human beings. We want to be true to
who we really are and act from the essence of our being.
We want to actualize in the world what we have deep
within us. For that to happen it is often necessary to
disturb what is there now. It involves change. Every so
often our deeper self pushes through and challenges the
way we lead our lives, creating a disturbance or crisis with
which we need to deal.

Abraham Maslow explained:

Let us think of life as a process of choices, one after
another. At each point there is a progression choice and
a regression choice. There may be a point towards
defense, toward safety, toward being afraid; but on the
other side there is the growth choice. To make the
growth choice rather than the fear choice a dozen times
a day is to move a dozen times a day towards self-
actualization.[1]

To make this growth choice, and to carry on making it, is one of the main objectives of inner leadership.

An important aspect of making the growth choice is to choose what we know to be best for us. This is what is most in line with our values and purpose. If we choose what goes against our deeper values and purpose, we set up internal conflicts that consume our energy.

The following is a dramatic example of someone who made the fear choice, not the growth choice, with disastrous consequences for both him and his company.

---

### CASE NOTES 12
### THE FEAR CHOICE = LOSE/LOSE

Jack Evans was 58 years old and the finance director of a small, publicly quoted design company of which I was a non-executive director. The chairman and chief executive, Richard, a forceful man who owned 40 percent of the equity, wanted to make an acquisition. He was used to getting his own way, and could be intimidating.

Before the board meeting where this issue was to be decided, I spoke to Jack. He agreed that the acquisition would be a disaster, but he was worried about opposing Richard. He was nervous that if he lost this job he would not find it easy to get another at his age, and he still had a long way to go to earn himself a decent pension. But he agreed to support me.

The board meeting eventually reached the point of decision on the acquisition. Richard proposed it strongly and made clear his determination to push it through. Sean, the operations director, immediately voted for the proposal. I voted against it, expressing my deep concerns. It came to Jack. He shuffled his papers, he looked uncomfortable, he paused and looked around the room, he opened his mouth – and he abstained. He had become paralyzed. He couldn't say yes and he couldn't say no. So he received no credit from Richard for supporting him and he went against what he knew the situation demanded.

The acquisition was made. It was a disaster. Jack lost his job and the whole company went into receivership within a year, putting 80 staff out of work and reducing the value of Richard's stake from £2 million to nil.

## RELUCTANCE TO CHANGE

We have a natural reluctance to disturb our known worlds, because it means abandoning the familiar for the unknown, which involves taking risks. American psychologist Andras Angyal wrote:

> Abandoning the familiar for the unknown always involves risks. When the changes are far-reaching or precipitous, they are bound to arouse anxiety. The view that [personal] growth is inseparable from anxiety is shared by practically all thinkers who have substantially contributed to our understanding of anxiety.[2]

The process of making the changes that help to uncover the unconscious parts of ourselves – themselves a response to anxiety – arouses anxiety, making the resistance to change stronger. We need to overcome this. Resistance can take many forms, which you need to look out for.

A useful starting point would be to look at any reluctance you may feel about working through this book. You may not make the time to do this work; you may invalidate its worth; you may say it is too difficult; you may say you do not understand it; you may say it is not relevant for you now. Just note these as possible resistances that are cutting across your purpose, the purpose you set for working through this book at the beginning.

Assagioli makes much of the fact that we deny our impulses for growth.[3] His reasoning is that the more we are conscious of positive impulses, the more shame we feel about our failure to express those impulses. For this reason, when doing this work we need to be accepting of ourselves and our limitations, do what we can and feel good about that.

This work requires you to be vigilant in relation to the messages you are giving yourself. Keep telling yourself that you are doing the best you are able to at any given moment. You are.

## THE ROLE OF CRISIS

Sometimes a crisis is the catalyst for moving out of the status quo, providing a way of learning. This crisis may come out of a series of disappointments, or an emotional shock such as bereavement or redundancy. It may be a moral crisis, based on feelings of guilt or remorse for a deed done or not done. It may be triggered by a new phase or role, or by a change in circumstances, like redundancy. It may come without any apparent cause.

*Just when you thought you had it all taped*

Such a crisis often does begin with a vague dissatisfaction or sense of lack, but not with anything material. It feels elusive and hard to pin down. This vague dissatisfaction is a stirring of our will (see Chapter 12). Things that once occupied our interest seem to fade in importance and lose their value. We may start to question things and look for meaning in our life and perhaps in world affairs.

People tend to misunderstand what is happening, see it as an aberration and, feeling alarmed, make increasing efforts to go back to 'reality', the old life. A conflict emerges between the feelings actually felt and the 'reality' of how the individual feels things should be, how they were before. This, if recognized, is a sign that it is time to take note of what is happening. It signifies a change that we can either learn to accept or continue to resist.

There are some common crises. The adolescent crisis is one of personal identity, finding our own persona and separating from our parents. Hence the wild clothes, the strong opinions and the body piercing. The midlife crisis is known in some form by most people who are in their forties and many still in their thirties. It is a crisis of internal identity. You may wake up one day and the world is not quite the same. It does not seem so fulfilling, or it lacks meaning. You may ask: 'What am I doing with my life? Is it serving any purpose?' And this is also why some say that life begins at 40, because our real self makes a push through and brings us closer to who we really are.

---

## CASE NOTES 13 – A TRANSITIONARY CRISIS

In the 1980s I had a good job in the City of London, earning more than most people I knew. I had a BMW and a four-bedroomed house in a leafy suburb. My work was varied, challenging and interesting.

One day I woke up and felt distinctly less interested. Something was not right, not satisfying. I had a number of MBA brochures and thought perhaps this would rekindle my passion for work and lead to new opportunities. But my heart was not in that. I was in a crisis. I had set up a lifestyle, a whole way of being, which fitted well with the expectations of my peers and my family. I had taken years to establish it and then, suddenly, it meant nothing to me. This felt very painful.

I sought counseling, to help me make sense of the situation. To be true to myself I knew I had to stop what I was doing. Eventually, I left my job. I set up as a consultant to work with ecological businesses. Initially I had no clients and no steady income, but at least the work appealed to my values. Through this I soon met somebody who told me about psychosynthesis. It sounded like what I was looking for. Within a few days I enrolled on a five-year training programme, and it changed my life. I had to get to know myself before I could work with clients, so I began to question and understand the mindsets and constituents that determined so much of my behavior.

A deep part of myself had disturbed me. My job had not changed: I had changed. For me, the meaning disappeared, to be replaced, later, by something deeper. My will was involved in disturbing my equilibrium so that I would question my life and perhaps choose something less familiar and less safe as a means of growing as a person. Fortunately, I heard it and responded to it.

I cannot imagine how resentful and depressed I would have become if I had resisted and stuck with my nine-to-five job, which no longer made my heart sing. The disturbance gave me a wonderful opportunity to review myself, my values, my purpose and my aspirations. Had it not been for that I would not be writing this book or doing my current work, which I find so fulfilling. But at the time it was a very difficult experience.

The crisis of meaning brought me to a state where I was able to free myself from elements of my life with which I had been heavily identified. I could see more clearly that I was making choices that no longer suited me. I no longer needed many of the luxuries I was working so hard to afford, or the security of full-time employment. The crisis brought to the fore my values and my life's purpose, enabling me to trade money for free time and security for personal satisfaction. I found a pessimistic part of myself that found reasons to keep things as they were. The values and purpose that came to the front then are those that underpin my life today. I had experienced a deep part of myself, my center of identity, from which I could make free choices about my life and my work.

You may find the thought of a transformative crisis worrying. It can be a painful, uncomfortable and disorientating experience. There is often a fear that such a disturbance will lead to a loss of identity or a change in personality. In fact, it enables us to identify with something deeper within ourselves. It often brings with it an awakening of conscience, when we question our own motivations, the sufferings of others, what justification there may be for inequalities, accompanied by feelings of guilt. It leads to a place where, through understanding, we can accept ourselves for who we are. It also puts us in contact with our values and purpose and gives us energy to do something about whatever is bothering us, a directional, mobilizing energy – our will.

In Case notes 1 on GCV, a previous crisis in his life had given Andrew an experience that was very useful in coping with the discomfort of making significant changes in his new organization. In fact, it was a crisis, brought on by his mistake in presenting his ideas as a *fait accompli*, that precipitated his modeling of the values that inspired so many people to support the transformation of the company.

Transformations are often less dramatic than this, and involve our conscious and purposeful participation. By being self-aware and willing to be open to seeing these disturbances, we can regulate our development to a greater extent. If our lives become too stuck in the comfort zone and we continue to ignore the messages being given to us, the part of us that is willing to grow will shout louder, and louder, until it is heard. Inner leadership helps you to hear the voices before they shout too loudly.

---

### CASE NOTES 14 – FROM CRISIS TO CHOICE

Phil had worked in production at a brewery for 23 years. He worked from 8 am until 4 pm, Monday to Friday. The company decided to change the production process. Phil was told he would now be working four 12-hour shifts one week and three the next, some of which would be at weekends.

Phil was persuaded to go along with this because he was afraid of losing his job. However, his old pattern was so deeply embedded and his whole life revolved so much around it that he couldn't cope with the change. He became severely depressed and took weeks off work.

Phil was forced to question many of his basic assumptions about life and work, about what was important to him. The changes had thrown his family life and his social relationships into disarray. He had to look at whether he could work the new shifts and still have what was important to him outside work. He had to come to terms with how much his identity was bound in with his work situation. With some creative thinking he was able to see how he could reorganize his life to make the new work fit his requirements, which were now much clearer to him.

He came out of the situation feeling renewed, because the crisis had driven him towards being able to make a proper choice, not out of fear but having assessed his life and the role his work played in it. He would have given the job up if he felt it was incompatible with the things he found important in life.

## ADAPTIVE CHANGE

Being a self-leader requires you to adapt your way of thinking, probably to adapt your attitudes and behaviors. It is not easy. You need to lead yourself through it. Heifetz and Laurie wrote in *The Work of Leadership*:

Adaptive change is distressing for the people going through it ... Rather than fulfilling the expectation that they will provide answers, leaders have to ask tough questions. Rather than protecting people from outside threats, leaders should allow them to feel a pinch of reality in order to stimulate them to adapt ... Instead of maintaining norms, leaders have to challenge the way they do business.[4]

This description of leadership is also a very good description of the frame of mind needed to become adept at inner leadership. We need to ask challenging questions of ourselves, and live through those questions without being drawn into quick answers. We need to feel the pinch of reality, and challenge the way we lead your lives and the way we do business, among other things. Having mastered these for ourselves, we can use them more easily in our external roles.

The practice of inner leadership requires us to be open to learning new things about ourselves. We learn about ourselves by being aware of ourselves. We can continually learn from those around us if we remain open to that. People we work with are trying to help us do a better job for them, albeit sometimes unconsciously and sometimes not very subtly or gracefully. If you want to know what is required of you as a leader, remain open to learning from others.  Watch and listen to the signals being sent to you. To do this, you need to have the inner strength to admit to yourself that you don't know everything, remaining flexible and vulnerable.

To change how we see ourselves, to admit that the future is unknown and uncertain, that we cannot rely on our past experience to respond anew to what is in front of us now, requires our will, our own inner source of power, which directs and regulates our resources and energies to align with our values and purpose. Many times I have asked you if you are willing to do the exercises in this book, to put you in touch with the part of yourself that says 'yes' or 'no' to something. That is important.

In working with people going through major changes in their work and their lives, an important part of my job is to see them through these low periods, when it looks like everything is going backwards. At GCV, Andrew could easily have given up at the end of that disastrous meeting when it looked as though his plans were in ruins. But he could see the value in what he was doing, his sense of purpose was strong, and these helped him contact his will to see him through.

Will then provides the means for the values and purpose to be realized, so strengthening them as their benefits begin to show. Lack of will creates enormous problems. So many ideas that are important for people and the world never come to fruition as a result of a lack of will, a lack of will to change, to disturb the status quo, to make the effort, to think things through. Passivity is the enemy of will. When we are active, we exercise our will. When we are passive, we allow it to atrophy. But like a muscle, it does not disappear completely and it can be built up again.

There is more on will in Chapter 12.

## SELF-ACCEPTANCE

To change, you need to be aware of your imperfections at the same time as accepting them. We have built a society today that is short on self-acceptance. We all have to be doing better all the time, have bigger jobs or grander homes, or be thinner or richer, smarter or more caring, or living up to the aspirational standards pumped to us through our television screens, perfect couples, perfect friends, forever happy, witty and loving. Many people don't know what it is like to be accepted just for who they are, with all their foibles, limitations and inconsistencies. This breeds a feeling of insecurity, which makes it difficult to do things for which we may be rejected by others, like standing up for our beliefs, making an unpopular decision or acting in a way that is congruous with how we feel.

As we learn to accept ourselves, our self-assurance becomes genuine, which means that we can take risks, because we can withstand the knocks to our egos and to our more flexible view of the world. Self-acceptance is the subject of Chapter 13.

# *Your Center of Identity* 10

Your center of identity has already been mentioned many times in this book, as itself, as the observer and as the conductor of the orchestra.

The center of identity has two main functions. It is the center of our awareness, the observer, enabling us to see ourselves in our entirety and within the context of our lives, and linking us with our purpose and values, bringing these into everyday life. It is the part that can see where we are aiming and where we are now.

*Link with our guiding principle*

But it also has a second function. The will, which directs and regulates our various functions in order that we may achieve what we want to, is also closely connected to the center of identity. It is the will that enables us to take energy away from a constituent or mindset to the center of identity and then to another constituent of our choice more aligned to our purpose.

## YOUR CENTER OF IDENTITY AS A UNIFIER

Your center of identity is like the conductor of an orchestra. She does not produce the musical sound, but

she embraces the whole, the music on the page, the instruments at her disposal and the type of performance. She directs the whole orchestra, bringing in each section as the music requires. The conductor directs her awareness not on herself, but on the orchestra and the music as it unfolds moment by moment. She uses her awareness and her will to bring the music into being.

*Integration of the parts*

As we learn to experience our center of identity, we become increasingly able to see ourselves as a whole entity, to separate ourselves from a situation, to make appropriate decisions, to free ourselves from habitual constituents and mindsets. The clarity of awareness and the direction of the will effectively harmonize the many elements within us to form a coherent and powerful whole, an integrated person. It becomes a unifying center around which we can organize aspects of ourselves to achieve what we want. It is where we find our essence and our spirit. When you experience your center of identity, you have the experience that you are more than the parts with which you normally associate yourself.

Warren Bennis recognized this when he said: 'the process of becoming a leader is the same as the process of becoming an integrated human being'.[1]

Because it is the central part of ourselves, the observer of all else, it is not possible to meet your center of identity full on. As it is the observer, if you can observe it, that is not it. You cannot be that which you observe. Like the Tao in ancient Chinese philosophy, if you can define it, that is not it.[2] However, you can experience it. By observing the parts of yourself you are experiencing it already. Exercise 19 in Chapter 11 will give you further experience of your center of identity.

Whereas a constituent is activated by a need, an urge or a desire, which you could say has a specific color, your center of identity does not contain a specific color. To stretch the analogy, it is white light, containing all the colors of the spectrum. It has no polar opposites, no distortions of itself. It is not moralistic or judgmental. It is the stable place from which you can regard and direct what is happening, with acceptance and clear perception. It is an observing center of awareness and volition, or will.

TS Eliot described the center of identity as 'the still point'.[3] It is still, but it is not fixed or stuck. It is the here and now, a point where we can live in the present and put the situation first. This still place is difficult to describe, and you know when you have been there. This place is free from desire, a release from suffering and compulsion. It is also unfettered by the things that get in the way when we are trying to see each situation clearly. But it is not entirely mystical either, it has a grace of sense, a connection to the real, practical world.

*Living in the here and now*

---

## CASE NOTES 15 – FINDING CLARITY

Jill was 42 and a single parent of a five-year-old daughter. She was an electrical engineer, working as a manager in product development for a large company designing and manufacturing environmental control systems. She was really struggling with life, with work, with being a single parent and with her finances, which showed in her work. She felt isolated and, as she put it:

> I was at the end of my tether. I had completely run out of ideas about what to do about my life. I felt exhausted. If I stopped working to cope with the rest of life, I could not survive financially. But working at the same time as trying to cope with everything else was killing me. I could not see my way forward. I was in a state of despair.

It sometimes happens when we reach rock bottom, a state of virtual surrender, that something does stir deep within us, the will to live or to improve life. Jill awoke one morning with a feeling of great clarity about herself and her life. She could see that she projected the anger she felt towards her ex-partner on to her boss, straining that relationship to its limits. She could see how she had chosen her ex-partner because he was similar in certain ways to her father, who had died when she was 12. She could see how she used the strains of work and parenthood to exclude herself from friends and family, which meant that no one was in a position to challenge her view of the world and the way she lead her life. It also meant that she received very little support. She remembered why she had chosen her field of work, how passionate she felt about it.

She could see how many things had come together to bring her to this point in her life where she was in crisis. She saw that her choice was not between her work and her child, but whether or not to take responsibility for her own life and try to live it to the full. She recognized the dominance of her victim constituent and how her attitude to life kept her in a position of isolation and powerlessness:

> I felt as though I was watching a screen on which all these aspects of my life, all these thoughts, relationships and dilemmas passed, like a film. I felt entirely calm. For the first time for months I felt I had space in which to think. It was as though everything moved away from me so I could see it. In that moment, I did not have to do anything except look. I felt very real and powerful.

Jill had experienced her center of identity. Her awareness of herself was raised, enabling her to observe her life in its context, without judging herself or wanting to push away its reality. Her will to grow as a person emerged, as shown in her willingness to enter counseling. From that point, she knew she could cope. She turned her identification away from the victim and powerlessness towards her will to achieve what she wanted in life. She had new-found enthusiasm for her work and soon gained promotion. This eased her financial pressures and enabled her to organize her home-life in the way she wanted it:

> I had almost given up hope that I could turn my life around, but I did. My boss was so relieved. He later confided that he was wondering if he had the guts to fire me at one point because he was so fed up with my outbursts.

Jill's experience of her center of identity was waking one morning to see exactly where she was in life. It came to her as a flash of insight, and she was prepared to listen. Examples of different experiences of the center of identity are described in this book. Deborah in Case notes 17 (Chapter 11) was able to stand back from her life and see clearly how she could use her own particular gift, which was precipitated by seeing the 'long shadow cast over her life'. This was her standing in her own center of identity. Also in Chapter 11, Derek is able to find a place where he can observe himself and keep coming back to his owl constituent.

## Exercise 18
## Experiencing your center of identity

It is important that you build up personal experience of your center of identity. This is so much more powerful than describing it. If you are willing, try some or all of these exercises to help with this.

- Hold a blank sheet of paper up in front of you. Who is looking at it?
- Make your own choices to do things you tend not to do out of deference to others, to say yes or no to requests, to eat what you want to eat, to wear what you feel like wearing, to express yourself creatively.

- Draw, paint or write whatever comes to you for 15 minutes. Observe yourself doing this. Monitor what is happening in your body, emotions and thoughts.
- Be discerning and decide whether or not you like things without finding out if they are supposed to be good, such as wine, or books, or films.
- Look at specific objects you have in your home and office. Do you like them still? What relevance do they have to you now? If you had to choose to let some go, which would be easy and which difficult?
- Consciously move from one constituent to another in a particular situation.
- Change one of your opinions.
- Examine your values and decide which are truly yours (see Chapter 7).
- Imagine ways of acting perfectly in line with your values and purpose (see Chapter 8)
- Practice being still. Sit in a comfortable position, with your eyes closed or in soft focus on an object. Observe the thoughts that pass through your mind without judging them or stopping them, remaining outside them.
- Practice the freeing exercise described in Exercise 19 (page 124).

## SELF-REALIZATION

Joseph Campbell, in *Myths to Live By*, quotes CG Jung as saying:

In the last analysis every life is the realization of a whole, that is, of a self, for which reason this realization can be called 'individuation'.[4]

Campbell goes on to explain:

The aim of individuation requires that one should find and then learn to live out of one's own center, in control of one's for and against. And this cannot be achieved by enacting and responding to any masquerade of fixed roles.

Realization, then, is finding and then learning to live out of one's own center. We achieve this by cutting through the fixed roles, the habits, the masks, the constituents, and facing each situation for what it needs. Your experience of your center of identity, as your unifying center, is a key part of your development towards inner leadership. To see yourself as you could be and to find the right steps to move from your present reality is a task that can be tackled step by step if you have the will to do so and the capacity to accept yourself as doing your best at any particular moment.

In *The Farther Reaches of Human Nature*, Maslow states:

Especially with adults we are not in a position where we have nothing to work with. We already have a start; we already have capacities, talents, directions, missions, callings. The job is to help them to be more perfectly what they already are, to be more full, more actualizing, more realizing in fact what they are in potentiality.[5]

*Being what we already are*

# 11 *Freeing Yourself from Constituents and Mindsets*

As we saw in Chapters 5 and 6, when we are strongly identified with one aspect of ourselves, much of our energy flows through that aspect and we are unable to identify with anything else.

In this chapter we will explore the idea of moving between our different constituents, employing the one that is most appropriate to any situation. Before this, I would ask you to try something.

Look around you and notice everything that is red, what it is and where it is placed. Now close your eyes and remember as many of the red things as you can. How did you do?

When you close your eyes again, recall all of the blue things around you. You probably can't remember very many. Then think of the red things again.

From this you can see the power of where we put our attention. Experiences that threaten our strongest identifications are played down. A mindset or a constituent has a quality about it, a color, which attracts other similar colors. Conflicting experience, other colors, begin to be invalidated and more energy is given to the constituent. It becomes a feedback loop, which is difficult to break.

For example, in a working situation, it is easy to be drawn in by whatever seems urgent at the time, by whatever is presenting itself to us in the most demanding way. Many leaders and managers tell me that they always seem to be firefighting. It is easy to be drawn into a crisis that needs to be solved. There are good payoffs. Firefighting is exciting, producing an adrenalin rush. It often has quick solutions and rapid and measurable results, providing a feeling of achievement. For these reasons, it is a favorite sport of management. However, it often leaves no time for the quiet reflection that could make firefighting less necessary. How often have I heard people say that they don't have the time to do the thinking they need to do, because they are rushing around doing other things, solving problems, organizing people, making themselves feel important?

Identification has its useful aspects. It enables us to concentrate on one thing for a period, because it is restrictive. When we identify with one part of ourselves, we can experience it fully. This is fine, as long as it is a conscious choice suited to the circumstances. For instance, if you are dealing with a client it may be better not to be in a leader role, but instead to meet them as a supplier, or as someone in their service, or as a salesperson.

## THE PROCESS OF BECOMING FREE

By being self-aware, practicing the attitude of the observer, we can see that we have an identification that has drawn in our energy, and we can see that it is not all we are. Going back to the example of firefighting, we could take a closer look at the nature of the problem. Is it really that urgent? Is there someone else who could handle it? Are we dealing with that because it is easier than planning a longer-term strategy, or putting together a marketing plan, or going to see a customer? Perhaps these tasks that are more behind the scenes do not appeal to our sense of who we are, as decisive, practical, action-oriented beings who 'get things sorted'.

*The owl, the frog and the bear*

---

**CASE NOTES 16
CHOOSING CONSTITUENTS**

Derek was 48 and worked as a structural engineer within an engineering consultancy. He was given the job of selling its services to the main contractor of a large and prestigious project to build a new road bridge. Derek was finding this difficult. His team was well qualified for the job, but was up against some solid competition and he did not feel that he had a close rapport with the contractor. Derek did not feel himself to be a very gregarious man. He tended to be introspective.

He had been using inner leadership mentoring for a year to help him regain enthusiasm for his work, which had waned in recent years. At his age, and as a partner within the consultancy firm, he did not feel inclined to move, but retirement seemed a long way ahead. Winning this contract would be an achievement he could be proud of, and running the project would be an exciting challenge.

Derek uncovered a number of constituents in the course of his inner leadership work. A lover of the natural world, he tended to use animals as symbols. He identified a grizzly bear, who could be protective of his beliefs in a rather dismissive and sometimes frightening, bullying way. He identified his most habitual constituent as a frog on a lily pad, isolated, looking and watching things happening but not involving himself. A third was an owl, sharp, intelligent and responsive, but not often visible. He associated the owl with wearing his glasses on the end of his nose.

Derek was asked by the contractor to present his firm's case. He knew that the contractor would not want a formal presentation, but instead would want to ask questions and discuss topics in detail concerning the experience and ideas of Derek's company. The contractors had a reputation for playing hardball during these meetings. Derek was asked to come alone, as the potential project leader.

He knew that he was in the hot seat in an unstructured situation. He did not entirely know what to expect. As a structural engineer he preferred known and quantifiable situations, so he felt exposed. As he described it: 'I felt more like a frog than an owl, and under pressure I was worried I would turn grizzly.'

Derek sat down at the table and was immediately confronted by a team of four technical people, who questioned him aggressively. He told me:

> I put my glasses on the end of my nose and conducted the entire proceedings from behind them. I was grilled for eight hours, with a new team being brought in every two hours. My attention was entirely focused on the job. My glasses reminded me all the time to act from the owl constituent. When I felt other constituents coming through, I remembered the owl. I answered every question coherently and satisfactorily. I felt sharply alive. I was really enjoying myself, and my enthusiasm came through. I was even humorous. We won the contract, one of the largest ever undertaken by my firm and one which led on to other work with the contractor. I felt so proud of myself. It was the first time I felt I had made a major contribution to the company for a number of years. My self-esteem rose and my enthusiasm for my work was rekindled.

Through making a positive identification with a constituent, Derek had managed to free himself from the more habitual ones. Note how he was able to observe himself and keep in the state he needed to be in to meet the situation. He could use his will to bring him back to this when he saw himself going away from it. His use of his glasses as a physical reminder was a good ploy.

In his book *Myths to Live by*, Joseph Campbell explains:

WHO COULD I BE TODAY?

> Just as every person consists of a head, a trunk, two arms etc. so does every living person consist of a personality, a deeply imprinted persona through which he is made known no less to himself than to others … To become – in Jung's terms – individuated, to live as a released individual, one has to know how and when to put on and to put off the masks of one's various roles. … But this is not easy, since some of the masks cut deep. They include judgment and moral values. They include one's pride, ambition and achievement. They include one's infatuations.'

These masks, the masks that cut deep, can often only be put on and put off with practice and awareness, and the will to do so.

## Exercise 19
## Freeing ourselves from identifications

A good way to learn to free yourself from identifications is to try it first with your body, emotions and mind. Sit in a comfortable position where you will not be disturbed.

Put your attention on to your body. Feel its state of relaxation or tenseness. Notice your breathing without trying to change it. Say to yourself: 'I have a body, and I am not my body. I am more than my body.' Your body is something that is changing. Cells are continually dying and being renewed. You can observe your body, so it cannot be all that you are. Repeat this three times: 'I have a body, and I am not my body. I am more than my body.'

The second stage is to put your attention on to your emotions. Really identify these. Are you feeling happy or sad, anxious or relaxed? What emotions are around you? Now repeat three times: 'I have emotions, and I am not my emotions. I am more than my emotions.'

Sometimes we do feel completely taken over by emotions, but there is always a part of ourselves that can stand outside of them, especially with practice. Strictly, instead of saying 'I am angry', it would be correct to say 'A part of me feels angry.' You may also recognize that there is a part of you that does not feel angry, that is seeking to understand, that wants reconciliation. The anger will pass with the event that caused it, or after a short time.

The third stage is to observe your thoughts. Watch them pass, like clouds across a sky. Do not try to change them. Do any seem habitual? Repeat three times: 'I have thoughts, and I am not my thoughts. I am more than my thoughts.' We often identify ourselves with our thoughts, but if we analyze them we see how often they change, and we can observe them if we practice.

The body, emotions and mind are instruments of experience, perception and action, changeable and impermanent. They serve you. They are not you.

As you practice this exercise, you can add in your strongest identifications. Remember what it is like to be identified with a constituent or mindset. Experience it in your body, emotions and thoughts. Then say 'I have <the name of your constituent>, and I am not <the name of your constituent>. I am more than that.' Doing this will give you some distance from the identification, and the choice to step out of it into something else.

If you practice this exercise for a few days, you will see that it has a subtle and profound effect on your attitudes and thoughts. You will see how often you do identify with parts of yourself. You will see that you can step out of them and that there is something else, your center of identity, which observes and directs with awareness and will. Many people find the exercise very calming, which can be useful in itself in this busy and stressful world.

Notice the effect of doing this exercise on your ability to experience your still point, your center of identity.

## Exercise 20
## Keeping the balloon in the air

Think of the things in your business life with which you most identify: maybe your position, your role, your expertise, your views, your knowledge, your office with a good view. Write these down on slips of paper.

Now, you are flying in a balloon that is gradually losing height, falling into the ocean. To save weight you must jettison those things with which you identify. Throw them overboard slowly, with awareness, one by one. Choose the ones you are most willing to let go of first. Are there things of which you are unable to let go? Complete this before you read on.

How did you feel doing this exercise? How difficult was it to let go of some things? Perhaps you found that there are things with which you identify strongly. Anyway, you can now have back all the things you threw out. The exercise was to see how identified you are with certain things. We do not need to be rid of our constituents, only aware of them.

---

**CASE NOTES 17**
**FREEDOM FROM IDENTIFICATION**

Deborah, aged 35, works in a large computer systems company, as a personal assistant to a department head. She felt that her job was not much more than being a 'paper shuffler'. She was unfulfilled, but could not see herself doing anything very different. From her position, the promotion prospects looked poor.

Deborah recognized that she was becoming increasingly irritable, especially at work. She often felt bored and unwell and was taking increasing amounts of sick leave. This gave her more time for reflection. She found that there was another part of herself of which she was catching glimpses, a part that wanted to get on and enjoy life. She had a good degree and at one time had envisaged herself getting a more high-powered job. Somewhere things seemed to have gone awry. There was some awareness within her that she was underachieving.

She went to see an inner leadership mentor. Through talking about herself, she remembered that her father had bullied and teased her from a young age and, as she put it, 'this had cast a long shadow over my life'. She had only vaguely remembered this before and had not recognized its lasting effect. As a result, she felt frightened to confront people and situations, believing that she would always come out worst and suffer humiliation. This meant that she tended to blame others and the outside world for her inability to feel fulfilled in life. She felt that there was always something blocking her, a glass ceiling, or a hostile manager, or even the fact that she was efficient in her work and her boss wanted to keep her where she was.

In her non-work life, Deborah felt restricted by how she perceived others saw her, by the hostile environment in her neighborhood and by 'them', some outside authority. She always seemed to be blaming the council, or the government, or the education system for things that went wrong in her life. These were manifestations of her inner world, which was protecting her from hurt and projecting her sense of powerlessness on to the outside world.

To cope with the narrowness in her life she had to repress aspects of herself that would lead her to more life-enhancing experiences. She always found a reason not to take the holiday she longed for, or not to apply for the job that might have given her a boost. Through this she was building a wall, keeping out the more adventurous part of herself in order to be satisfied with her restricted state. Of course, at this stage she was not conscious of all this. She just saw it as the way things are. It seemed normal to her.

*Recognizing*

*Exploring*

Through her mentoring work Deborah began to explore what she believed about herself. She saw more clearly within herself a constituent that was cautious and unadventurous, which held her back by continuing to cast the 'long shadow' over her life. She called this constituent 'young Cinderella', because she was always at the beck and call of others, of the demands of life, her 'ugly sisters'. Having recognized this and explored what lay behind it, she was also able to recognize the part that wanted to get on, her 'Ms Go-Ahead'. Now that she could see both, the possibility of choosing not to play young Cinderella opened up.

Looking at herself closely, with more optimistic eyes, she could recognize qualities that she had not clearly seen before and realize that her values of fairness and loyalty are important to her. Through this process of exploration, she came to see herself as a powerful and competent woman capable of much more than she had been achieving. Studying her qualities and skills, she concluded that she would make a good manager. She now knew that she had to listen to her 'fairy godmother', believe in herself and be willing to step out into the world.

*Actualizing*

Feeling more confident now, and much to the surprise of her boss, Deborah asked to be placed on a management training course. She was surprised by the strength of her determination to make this happen. Ms Go-Ahead and her will were active (the will is featured in Chapter 12). Following the course, Deborah gained promotion, supervising a team of six people responding to inquiries on a customer helpline. In her work she aims to 'bring out the best in people and be a manager in my own particular gift'. She sees her gift as being intuitive, able to see people's qualities and what they are good at, and really wanting to help them to develop.

Deborah was reflecting the process through which she had taken herself in her mentoring. Her values

strengthen her resolve to be a good and fair manager.
She believes that a happy and secure workplace
makes for an efficient one in which people can function
to the best of their abilities. She knows how
debilitating fear can be. If people feel confident, they
treat their customers with patience and respect,
sorting out problems more quickly. She is introducing
her staff to the principles of inner leadership, because
she has found it useful herself. She views it as
engendering an atmosphere of trust and openness.

Deborah could see that some managers in the
company behaved like bullies, lowering the self-
esteem of their staff, who then tended to complain
among themselves and 'turn off' from trying to do a
good job. She recognized that they fell into the victim
mode that she used to experience. She decided to do
something about this, to take the lead to change
things:

*Leading*

I persuaded the department head to introduce an
item on management policy and values on to the
agenda of all management meetings, to bring
regular discussion which would determine how
managers are expected to behave. I used my skills
to introduce the concept of fostering open
relationships as a basis for management. I
developed the idea of 'optimum fit', by which I
mean matching the skills of people to tasks and
providing the time for training to fill competence
gaps.

Deborah used self-awareness and a greater
understanding of her internal processes to free herself
from her identification with her past experience and
her restrictive self-image. By doing this, she became
able to see her skills and qualities from the
perspective of what she wanted to achieve in her life.
She has transformed her 'wound' into her 'own

**Connecting inner to outer**

particular gift' and passed what she has learned on to others. She has achieved transformation by elevating the reactive, pleasing behavior of young Cinderella into a willingness to serve others at the same time as achieving her own aims. Ms Go-Ahead and young Cinderella are combining their talents. So Deborah is able to serve without being a victim, without demeaning herself, and she is able to get on without losing touch with her values and who she is. The idea of finding an 'optimum fit' is an external version of her own ability to match her own strengths and qualities to the challenges in her life.

Deborah has gained herself a reputation as someone who is thoughtful about management and who takes it seriously. She has improved the effectiveness of her own team and improvements are coming through in the department as a whole. She has had to be strong enough to withstand hostility from managers who did not like her ideas. Deborah's aim now is to find herself a broader role where she can concentrate on improving leadership and management within the organization.

What Deborah has achieved is an important element of inner leadership. She has understood her internal world and been able to apply her new insights in her work situation. She is taking the lead. Imagine the multiplier effect when you have a number of Deborahs in an organization, bringing their self-awareness and their greater trust of themselves and others together. They form high-performance teams.

## Exercise 21 – Breaking free

Using Case notes 17 on Deborah as an example, trace the development of one of your constituents or mindsets and your identification with it. You could use your work from Exercises 6 and 7 in Chapter 5 on constituents or Exercises 10 and 12 in Chapter 6 on mindsets, or you could find a new one. Write the story of it as fully as you can. See where it is in its development, how it affects you, how it benefits you and limits you.

Now think of what it might be like to be able to free yourself from this mindset or constituent. Write this as a semi-fictional case study, based on real aspects and circumstances of your life, but using your imagination to move beyond where you are with it now. Consider what effect this would have on your life, your work, your ability to take the lead and to achieve what you want to achieve.

Now consider whether it feels viable for you to do this. What might be the difficulties you need to overcome? How willing are you? Think of ways in which you could overcome the difficulties, remembering that some of these could be part of your unconscious defense mechanisms to avoid changing.

Note how you feel in tackling this exercise, in your body, emotions and thoughts. What are you learning from this about yourself and your attitude to change?

# *12* *Your Will*

Our will is an internal directive force, the power that enables us to actualize who we truly choose to be. It is our will to grow. It gives us the power to be autonomous, to act according to our purpose and our values.

There are times when we do something, but we are not sure why. This action turns out to be important, to help put us on a path towards something of significance. It is only later that its relevance becomes conscious. In these cases our will precedes our consciousness. It is a carrier of messages from deep within ourselves into conscious action.

The will is much misunderstood today, as something enabling us to do things we don't want to do, such as diet. That is 'willpower'. Or people who have 'strong will' are seen to be bullying, imposing their will on the rest of us in a win/lose battle. Or people who are 'willful' are often seen to be selfish or obstructive. These are distortions of our real will, which stands in service of our ultimate purpose and values. It is part of our center of identity, part of the conductor of the orchestra. Our will is a hugely positive force in our lives, both in personal and collective terms. Its place in inner leadership needs to be understood.

*Strong will* is the most familiar embodiment to many people. In strong will lie the power and the energy to generate enough intensity to carry out its purpose.

*Skillful will* uses our psychological energies to help us and develops strategies entailing the greatest economy of effort. Skillful will is not a direct power or force, but is the function at our command to stimulate, regulate and direct all the other functions and forces of our being towards achieving our purpose. It uses imagination, intuition, thought, feelings, impulses and sensations.

There is also *goodwill*. This takes into account the relationships, interactions and working associations that will block us from our purpose if we oppose them. It is the will to be cooperative and collaborative, aimed at harmonizing the wills of all concerned. Goodwill enables us to align our own purpose with other, broader aims and purposes.

SKILLFUL WILL

Use of our will brings us the courage to stand resolutely for what we believe in, even if it would be easier to back down. It enables us to respond to our calling, to what is important to us, to gather all our resources and make the decision that, in our heart of hearts, we know we should make. It is our will that enables us to step out of the comfort zone and make the growth choice.

## THE WILL IS DIRECTIVE AND REGULATORY

Our will helps us to give structure and meaning to our lives and motivation to our actions. It may be in the small voice urging us to do something, the hunch or the insight. The central aspect of working with the will consists precisely in being aware of what we are going to do and how we are going to do it. We act from an inner clarity of purpose rather than out of a desire, need or urge.

Assagioli described the will as having 'a directive and regulatory function; it balances and constructively utilizes all the other activities and energies of the human being'.[1]

*The will and clarity of
purpose*

Along with awareness, it is one of the two parts of the center of identity, the conductor of the orchestra. The conductor needs awareness, of the music, of the atmosphere and the sound she wants to create, of the means disposable to her, but she also needs the will to make it happen, to keep the rhythm, to bring in the instruments, to actualize the performance. She brings together and directs the energies of the orchestra to bring the music to life, taking it from the page to the performance.

Assagioli also described the will as the helmsman of a sailing ship, who knows its course and makes adjustments to counteract the forces of the wind and the current. The power the helmsman needs to turn the wheel is not the same as that needed to propel the ship through the water, which is more akin to the Victorian concept of strong will. By developing the will we can improve the effect of all future endeavors.

---

## CASE NOTES 18
## DAVID'S STORY – THE WILL IN ACTION

'Visiting a friend I had not seen for some time, I spoke of a sense of dissatisfaction with my work: for 14 years I had been a director and shareholder in a successful and prestigious IT systems company which bore my name. My friend asked, "What is it you really want to do?" I replied without hesitation, "I want to be a psychologist." And this was the first I had heard of any such ambition. She responded, "Well, that's very interesting, because I have been doing this course in psychosynthesis…"

'This incident coincided with a crisis of meaning in my life. Soon after, I gave my business partners two years' notice of my intention to end my career in IT in order to enter some form of psychology training. I also enrolled on a basic course in psychosynthesis, similar to inner leadership but without the specific business focus.

'A year on and plans to sell my shares, introduce an external financial partner and prepare the company to go to the next level were maturing well and we had stimulated a lot of interest. Then Saddam Hussein invaded Kuwait. Borrowing rates soared, peaking at 20 percent. Business confidence plummeted. Potential investors trickled away. Our largest single contract was part of a major strategic project in the Arab world. The Gulf War created contractual difficulties for this project, which impinged on our subcontract, where much of our working capital was tied up. Our cashflow position was tight, but we remained solvent.

'Given the circumstances, we did everything right. We made our plans to batten down the hatches and weather the storm, including making one-third of our staff redundant (a sad day) and moving to smaller offices. We had always had a close relationship with our bank, and as always we appraised them of our plans, including the appointment of an administrator for a short period to dispose of the leases on our premises and surplus vehicles. At the mere mention of an administrator the bank went into spasm. They condemned the company to immediate receivership without discussion or appeal. Subsequent mismanagement by the receivers transformed the company's solvent state into a substantial loss which by dint of guarantees was laid at the directors' door.

'Prior to these events I had been the eponymous director of a successful IT systems company with considerable prestige, an enviable reputation in the industry, an illustrious and loyal client base, and a well-proven record of technological achievement, inventiveness, efficiency and quality. I was a man of considerable reputation and standing.

'Now it had all gone. I had no job. I had no money, only a then incalculable debt. I faced the threat of losing my home. I had no pension, for that was to have come from the sale of shares. I had no reputation or status, for there is no one lower than a director of a company in receivership. I even felt I had lost my name, for the company had been given my name and now it no longer existed.

'But, when everything was stripped away, and for the first time in my life, I knew who I was. I had a clear and tangible sense of my own identity. It is not easy to describe this experience, but amidst all the fear and grief there was also exultation. It was like I had lost everything but had found the pearl of great price.

*Crisis brings a sense of identity*

'I have no doubt that this sense of identity was crucial to the directing of my will in the days following. The main task was to sell off what we could of the company's operations in order to save as many jobs as possible. The industrial systems side of the company had some synergy with a company I had been dealing with for some time, so I pointed my partners in that direction and they successfully negotiated a sale; in fact, that operation continues to trade today. I concentrated on selling the financial systems side, successfully as it turned out, to some other IT services company. We saved about two-thirds of the remaining jobs.

'I knew I had only two weeks in which to dispose of the financial systems operation, while the corpse was still warm. Amidst the frenetic activity, stress, dread, anxiety, heartache and endless faxes, phone calls and meetings during those two weeks, two incidents stand out in my memory.

'The first is a Saturday visit to a client company in Northern Ireland. On the plane over I felt like death. I felt all in pieces, possessed by grief and fear. Little by little during the flight I seemed to gather my inner resources. My host met me at Aldergrove and took me to his offices in Antrim where a group had gathered to meet me. Speaking and acting out of those inner resources, I argued my business case and presented my ideas with complete focus, passion, humor, and conviction. When my host returned me to the airport, he shook my hand warmly and looking me straight in the eye he said in his Belfast brogue, 'You are a courageous man.' Leaving him, I went and sat in the bar with a pint of Guinness and wept my heart out.

'The second is a visit to the director of an international IT services corporation, who was responsible for their IT systems and consultancy business in the UK. Waiting for the London train, I met an acquaintance who, though he had a first-class ticket, volunteered to travel with me in second class. I was awful, sounding off with dogmatic opinions about anything and everything – as we passed the recently renamed Forte Hotel I went on about 'bloody Fawlty Towers'. Awful. Looking back, I suppose this helped me get rid of a lot of surplus and fragmentary emotional energy, so that I was able to present my business case to the director I was visiting with calm assurance and was able to relate to him with patience and restraint, which is what was needed in this case.

'I went on to rebuild my IT systems career and worked for another eight years as a financial and business systems consultant. These proved to be the most successful and satisfying years of my whole IT career. I made more money than I had ever made in my life. I paid off my debt to the bank. I funded and completed seven years of psychology training, gradually scaling down my IT work in order to maintain a balance between my need for income and my need to satisfy the rigorous demands of the training.

'I now have an MA in Psychosynthesis. I am in practice as a fully qualified, professional psychotherapist.'

*Meeting the real needs of the situation*

David's unexpected declaration that he wanted to be a psychologist, which surprised even him, coinciding with the fact that his friend could provide him immediately with a relevant course that captured his imagination, is typical of the way the will works to make the inner voice audible and to provide a means of response to that voice.

David had been taken out of his comfort zone. Having decided to take things at a sensible pace and do them in an ordered fashion, he was now catapulted into a new situation over which he appeared to have much less control. He was in the midst of a crisis. He had understandable grounds to feel victimized, angry and resentful. And yet...

David's world had been upset by his declaration that he wanted to be a psychologist and by the events affecting the sale of his company. He had a plan worked out, but it went awry. Had his plan not gone wrong, he would not have been involved in the most exciting and most lucrative part of his IT career. He told me that his original business had been successful, but not as successful as it could have been because he needed a large trade partner, but had not been prepared to relinquish control. Events forced him to let go, which turned out to be best for developing the business and for him personally.

Despite all that had happened to him, David retained a clarity of focus and a strength that enabled him to function in a remarkable way. We often flee from people in desperate straits: they remind us too much of our own vulnerabilities, Or we pity them. David elicited neither of these responses. He was taken seriously. He was given time. He was seen as courageous, which he certainly was. The will directs and regulates. It balances and constructively utilizes all our other activities and energies. For the most part David was in full command of his own powers, able to take charge of himself and be in control of the situation.

Many people who reach high positions in organizations have a great deal of strong willpower. They are prepared to work long hours, to put the company's needs before their own, make sacrifices and act skillfully to climb the ladder to corporate success. But they may not be using much of their will, connected to their center of identity, values and purpose. Often your will requires you to be creative and to take risks, to follow your hunches and do the right thing even if it seems difficult at the time. The action needed to produce outstanding results may not in fact require a huge effort. Often it feels like going with the flow.

## Exercise 22 – Do you use your will?

Think about the following questions in relation to your will. Use them to think of specific instances when you have used your will, and when you have not. Remember how each felt and the consequences for you and for others.

Jot down words that describe your feelings when you have used your will, and when you have not, so that you can contrast them.

- When you are given the opportunity to give your view and you feel it is right, but you are in the minority.
- When you are faced by an overwhelming task.
- When you are required to make a difficult decision and take action.
- When you could use an old solution or find a new one.
- When you are asked to do something you really don't want to do.
- When a situation is compromising your values.
- When there are distractions to take you away from your purpose.
- When you have a hunch or an idea.
- When you know you could express yourself creatively.

## Exercise 23 – Intensify your will

You can intensify your will by exercising it. Over the coming weeks, try some or all of the following exercises, remembering that the function of the will is to direct, not to impose:

- Make a plan and then follow it through.
- Say no when it is right to, but easier to agree.
- Do something or talk to someone you have been avoiding.
- Make a decision without hesitation (starting with minor ones).
- Remain quiet and reflective in a meeting where you are tempted to say a great deal.
- Find a way to achieve something with the minimum effort on your part.
- Perform an action with complete attention, as if it were your last.

You may find you experience some resistance to doing these exercises. Don't worry about that. Observe it. See how you feel, how you react physically, what thoughts come in, and bring yourself gently back to the task. If this is difficult, remind yourself of your purpose for embarking on it. Don't judge yourself.

---

The exercises throughout this book require your will. Practicing them is an excellent exercise that is self-enforcing, because the will directs the play of various aspects of ourselves from an independent standpoint. It organizes us to live our values and reach our aspirations. It comes from our higher unconscious through our center of identity. It is our essence in action. The will finds the easiest and most skillful way through something, not the most arduous. If something feels like very hard work, then your will is not being fully used. That is not to deny that there are times requiring great effort and a strong push towards our goal.

If you want to strengthen your will, you could also practice Exercise 5 for developing qualities, found in Chapter 3.

## STAGES OF THE WILL

Using your will to achieve your purpose according to your values requires a systematic process. According to

Assagioli,[2] there are six sequential stages in using the will.
These are:

1  Purpose or aim based on evaluation, motivation and
   intention.
2  Deliberation.
3  Choice and decision.
4  Affirmation.
5  Planning and working out.
6  Direction of the implementation.

## Exercise 24 – Using your will to lead

1  **Purpose.** Define a purpose, something you would like to
   achieve, on which your will can operate. Preferably, your
   purpose will be in alignment with your values. Evaluate its
   importance and its achievability in relation to your skills,
   qualities and experience. You feel highly motivated when
   your purpose seems achievable and is aligned to your values
   and in service of something important to you.

2  **Deliberation.** Think now about ways in which you could
   achieve this purpose. In this stage of the process, immerse
   yourself in data and research and form your options for
   achieving what you want. Consider a variety of options. It is
   important at this stage to hold off from making a decision,
   which can be frustrating. Generate as many options as you
   can, trying not to shut down the less rational ones. When
   you are using your will and letting in new ideas, the
   unconscious mind is able to operate. This is when you might
   have an 'aha' experience. There may be something very
   creative there you have not thought about. There is a strong
   tendency in work situations to generate one or two choices
   and to act too quickly, before the deeper, more creative ideas
   have had an opportunity to emerge.

3  **Choice.** Now, using all the options and the data you have,
   you can choose a way forwards to achieve your purpose,

which is right for you and which is in alignment with your values.

4  **Affirmation.** It is important to affirm this choice so that you strongly give yourself the message that this is what you have chosen. It is useful to write it down and keep it in a prominent place so that you can refer back to it. Telling someone about your decision is a good way of affirming. You can make the affirmation more positive by telling yourself it is something you are in the process of achieving. Keep repeating this. The message enters your unconscious mind, which can then help you.

5  **Planning.** As with many business tasks, planning exactly how you are going to achieve your purpose, working out precisely how to put your decision into action, is a vital step.

6  **Implementation.** What is important here is the direction of the implementation. Keeping in mind your purpose and your values throughout the process will improve your motivation when things get tough. You only use means that serve the intended purpose. With your increased self-awareness, you are able to see more clearly the impact of your actions, how you feel about what you are doing, your own resistance and the parts of yourself that can be helpful. You may also find you are less inclined to feel you have to achieve everything yourself through sheer willpower. Rather, you can use your skillful will to utilize whatever resources you can make available, as well as goodwill to gain the cooperation of others, rendering successful implementation more likely.

# *Self-Acceptance* 13

Self-acceptance is very important for our self-development, if we are going to step out of the comfort zone and make growth choices. We are aiming to have available as much of ourselves as possible, to be used at will and when appropriate. We need to accept all parts of ourselves as valid.

Most of us have a strong tendency to criticize and judge ourselves for not being good enough, for lacking something, for being unworthy or incompetent. We are complex beings, and therefore there is a great deal of scope for our parts to be in conflict. Our dominant constituents and mindsets, which are semiautonomous, try to push out other parts so that they can reign supreme.

**FORGET PERFECTIONISM**

None of us is perfect, nor do we need to be. Perfectionism is a problem in many organizations. It keeps people away from the risk of being wrong, of failing, which seriously limits creativity. The following quote from George Soros, originally written about the drugs problem in the US, is equally applicable to us and to organizations as to society:

We act on the basis of imperfect understanding and our actions have unintended consequences. Our mental constructs, as well as our institutions, are all flawed in one way or another. Perfection is unattainable, but that is no reason to despair. On the contrary, our fallibility leaves infinite scope for innovation, invention and improvement. An open society that recognizes fallibility is a superior form of social organization to a closed society that claims to have all the answers.

## ACCEPTING ALL YOUR PARTS

It is so easy to judge ourselves as not being good enough, to criticize ourselves for our shortcomings and to compare ourselves with other people. Notice how often you do this both at work and at home. As you increase your self-awareness, you may find that at first you become increasingly self-critical. As you set yourself higher goals and attempt to live according to your values, you may feel even more acutely your failure to match your expectations. Don't despair.

In fact, through this work you can learn to take life and yourself more lightly. This does not imply being irresponsible, but rather keeping your sense of humor and your sense of joy, especially in adversity. I know for myself that 'sense of humor failure' is a prime indicator that I am not holding things lightly, that my ego is involved, that I have become identified with something, and that I need to find a way to let go.

Value yourself for taking on the task. If you work through this book you are doing something important. You are taking the risk of looking at your deep assumptions and how you really are, which will be uncomfortable and challenging at times. Appreciate yourself for doing this.

Now would be a good time to go back to Exercise 4 on recognizing your qualities in Chapter 3. Reassess how you see yourself given the depth of awareness and understanding of yourself that you now have. You may recognize that you have all of the qualities listed there, and many more not listed. If you have one quality, you also have its opposite. So you may as well accept yourself as having them all, as being capable of displaying any of them. You cannot know how creative you are, unless you know what it is like to be uncreative.

In the words of Lao Tzu:

> If all on earth acknowledge the beautiful as beautiful
> then thereby the ugly is already posited.
> If all on earth acknowledge the good as good then
> thereby is the non-good already posited.
> For existence and non-existence generate each other.
> Heavy and light complete each other. Long and short
> shape each other.
> High and deep convert each other. Before and after
> follow each other.[1]

Ultimately, you have the choice of which qualities, values and purpose you want to live by. Inner leadership increases your level of choice.

Accept every part of yourself. Every aspect of yourself has had a reason for being there at some time in your life. Take responsibility and own these parts of yourself. This will not have the effect of making them more dominant; in fact, it will do just the opposite. What does someone do when they feel they are being ignored? They repeat themselves, louder and louder, until they are heard. If that doesn't work, they will find some more dramatic way of expressing themselves.

*Unaccepted parts have power*

It is the same with our constituents, our emotions and our thoughts. If they are pushed away and ignored, they clamor for more attention. If they are listened to and accepted, they become quiet, no longer needing to push themselves forward inappropriately. Children show us this very clearly. If you ignore a child, she will repeat her claim until she has your attention. If the quality of that attention is poor, she will demand more of it. If you listen and give complete attention, even for a moment, so that the child feels heard and understood, she will be satisfied and move on.

Listen out for the judgments and criticisms you make about parts of yourself. If there are some that are particularly strong, try the following exercise.

# Exercise 25 – Self-acceptance

Write down your criticism. What is it and at which part of yourself is it directed? Make sure that it is not directed at your whole self. Be specific. For example, if you criticize yourself for being disorganized, state it in terms of criticizing the part of yourself that is disorganized, recognizing also that there is a part of yourself that is organized. Make the criticism of the part of yourself forcefully, speaking to it directly.

For example, you may say: 'I hate the way that you, the part that is so disorganized, leave tasks undone for days. My office is a mess. I don't complete my work on time. It takes twice as long as it should to get anything done'. Write down what is wrong with this part, what it should do and what it should not do. Tell it how it affects you.

*Criticisms are made by constituents to constituents*

Who is making the criticism? It will not be your center of identity; it will be a constituent. If I criticize the part of myself that is disorganized, it may be my diligent worker constituent who makes the criticism. It may be the internalized voice of my father or mother. What is important here is to know that the criticism is made by another constituent. The part being criticized is not all of you, and neither is the part making the criticism.

Now take the part of the criticized constituent. Answer the criticisms. What do you say in response? How do you feel about being criticized? How do you feel as you have the opportunity to answer the criticisms? Write all this down.

For example, my disorganized part may respond at first by apologizing, making excuses and feeling bad about itself. Let the critical part hear that. As this process continues, it may continue by pointing out that it is not necessary to be totally organized all the time, and that to be able to deal with chaos is a risk that takes courage. It is from this disorganized, chaotic part that real creativity is able to spring as I step outside my rational way of being.

Carry this on as a dialogue between the two parts. See if you can really get them to listen to each other and understand each other's point of view. In this example, it may be that the diligent worker fears chaos, or feels threatened by being out of control. When we do criticize parts of ourselves, it is often as a result of fear.

When you have finished doing this, review what happened. You may have experienced some kind of conflict, some division between a powerful, critical and authoritative part and a less powerful part. It may be as though you are divided into a parent and child or a top-dog and under-dog. Perhaps the critical voice is reminiscent of a real parent or authority figure from your earlier life.

As these two parts are able to listen and understand each other, what happens? Does the dialogue turn into animosity and the conflict become greater, or does it become difficult to keep the criticism going as understanding is increased? If the animosity increases, go back into the dialogue and try to get the two parts to listen to each other more carefully.

*The disagreement is within you*

It is important to realize here that all this is going on inside yourself. It is between different parts of yourself. As the dialogue continues, especially if the conflict is great, you may find that a third element is at work, attempting to create harmony, encouraging the two to understand and be compassionate towards each other. If its energy is clear and calm, that will be your center of identity. It provides a third point to bring integration. That point is your purpose.

For example, there may be a reason to accept both the disorganized, chaotic part of yourself and the diligent worker, once it is seen that both the creative chaos and the ordered environment are necessary to achieve your purpose, such as writing a book. This is not a compromise, to become less organized and less creative in order to meet somewhere in the middle. That would lead to mediocrity, giving the worst of both worlds. The transformation is to give your creativity enough organization to enhance its chances of coming to fruition. It is the purpose that encourages this to happen, the purpose of creating a book.

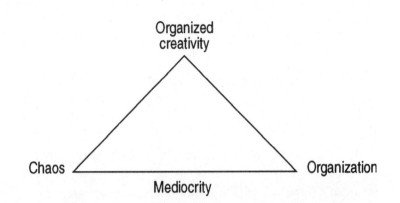

This is a powerful exercise, so treat yourself with care when you use it. Also, imagine how it would be to listen and to be listened to with this intensity when you are in conflict with somebody else. It shows how powerful it is if you make sure you understand somebody else before you make judgments about them. Try this in your role as a leader.

## ACCEPTING YOURSELF ENGENDERS EMPATHY

Your progress in inner leadership will be impeded if you cannot accept yourself for all you are. Only by accepting yourself can you treat others in the same way, with compassion and understanding, accepting their foibles and differences as being of value and a part of how they are, not something to try to fix and change. When you understand someone else as a whole person, like you, with internal conflicts and contradictions, with hopes and aspirations and frustrations and disappointments, it is hard not to respect them, accept them, love them. This does not mean that you then cannot be tough and frank with them; in fact, just the opposite. You can put a level of honesty into the relationship that would normally be difficult.

*We criticize to feel 'right'*

I can remember many instances when I have jumped to conclusions about people and their motives, without waiting for an explanation, only to regret it. It makes a part of me feel right and justified. I do it particularly with punctuality, berating people in my mind for being late.

This allows the part of me that is punctual, a dominant part, to feel virtuous and organized, and therefore good about myself. Often it is more the part of me that feels undervalued that takes offense when people are late, saying 'if they respected me they would arrive on time'. When the person arrives and I find out why they are late, there is frequently an unavoidable and plausible reason. I may also think about how little effect their lateness really had on me. Then the feelings of frustration and impatience disappear.

Many people are afraid that if they understand too much of the other person's position, they will not be able to push to get things done. How can you press a piece of work on to somebody if you know they are worried about their marriage and need to spend time working on that, which means leaving on time each evening and not working at weekends?

But think about this. If you do force work on someone in these circumstances, their personal position will deteriorate. They will resent you, even blame you for helping to wreck their marriage. Their output is likely to be below standard, and you will wonder why, become more frustrated and exacerbate the situation.  If you know what is happening for that person and are aware of their short-term limitations, you can work around that, plan for support, keep a closer eye on what is happening, perhaps even provide them with an external counsellor, or suggest it. They will then feel much more like extending themselves to do their manageable share of the work, will be less pressurized, feel they have a caring employer, look for solutions to the problem and are likely to be back to speed quicker. The understanding you have between you will act as common ground from which you can work together. Your relationships with people will improve dramatically.

I remember being struck when I was doing my psychosynthesis training how everyone had a life story worth listening to, how noble and special each person seemed once I knew them deeply. Everyone is worthwhile

*Understanding brings choice*

for who they are. I could see this more and more as I came to accept myself. Although I did not get on personally with everyone in that group, I was able to respect and love them for who they were. As Maslow states:

> You can certainly communicate better with a friend who is appreciated and understood than you can with a feared, resented and mysterious enemy. To make friends with some portion of the outside world, it is well to make friends with that part of it which is within yourself.[2]

One is a reflection of the other, a coming together of the inner and the outer.

## Exercise 26 – Listen before speaking

Practice this in your organization and in your personal life. When you find yourself being critical and judgmental of somebody, hear what they have to say. See if you can really understand their point of view. Listen, listen, listen. Be curious and ask questions. Check out that you have understood by trying to summarize what they have said to you. Reflect on what they have said, without judgment. Then, in the light of that, say what you want to say.

Make sure you start your sentences with the word 'I' and not 'you'. How different it is to receive 'I feel frustrated by...' than 'You are so frustrating...' Starting sentences with the word 'I' means that you are taking responsibility for your own state, for your own feelings. State how you see things, from your point of view, calmly and gently and without criticizing the other person. You will find that you now have a basis for collaboration.

This is not always easy to do. When you feel angry with somebody, it is difficult not to heap blame on them, accusing them of making you feel as you do, using emotive words like 'ridiculous' and 'stupid'. You may think you are using 'ridiculous' in relation to the situation, but in reality it is directed at the person. If you say 'that's a ridiculous way to go about something', you are really saying you think the person who chose to do it that way is ridiculous. That will put them on the defensive and the situation will enter a downward spiral.

*Stage 4*
# Leading

L EADING
A ctualizing
E xploring
R ecognizing

You are now ready to take the lead in whichever aspect of your life and work you choose. In this final part we bring all the elements together in order to be able to meet the real needs of each situation with awareness, aptitude and purpose. This part is about integration, about the balance and synthesis of difference. In order to be creative in our lives, we need the ability to transform ourselves by including all our qualities and our conflicting parts.

We will do this by creating a project in which you can combine all the elements. We will then look in the final chapter at some of the possible benefits of being a self-leader.

# *Self-Leading* 14

## RESPONDING TO THE REAL NEEDS

*Inner leadership allows you the clarity to respond to the real needs of a new situation with awareness, aptitude and purpose.*

Having worked through the book, you are now more able to trust yourself to make the best decisions you can. You can encourage participation and listen to other ideas and don't need to be attached to your own. You can be committed to the cause and remain objective at the same time. You can see change as non-threatening, and so be able to initiate and support it. As we near the end of the process, I hope you now have the confidence to practice 'courageous leadership' and act with full honesty and integrity. You can take personal responsibility and risks appropriate to the situation, because there is no reason to do anything else.

The ground has been prepared for this. You have learned more about yourself than is the case with most people. You know about your previously unconscious beliefs, attitudes, habits and norms. Able to experience your center of identity, you can free yourself from your habitual constituents when it is appropriate to do so. You can see more of yourself in the context of reality. You are more aware of your qualities. You can look beyond yourself, beyond the narrowness of your constituents and mindsets, to see the bigger picture. You are aware of your values and your purpose, providing yourself with a guiding principle. You are able to exercise your will and you see the importance of self-acceptance. You will now learn how to create results that look after your own needs for success and fulfillment at the same time as meeting the needs of the situation.

## TRANSFORMATION TO MEET REAL NEEDS

At this stage in the process of becoming self-leaders, we turn our minds from learning inner leadership to its practice in the outside world, in our organizational lives and wherever else we choose. We turn to the practice of seeing the real needs of situations and responding to them with awareness, aptitude and purpose. Your increased self-awareness is the key to being able to see the real needs of situations, by increasing the information you have and by being able to separate your inner reality from outer reality. Deeply knowing yourself as a whole, and the many parts of you including your values and purpose, enables you to see where you stand in relation to a situation.

But how do you move from here to responding to that situation's real needs? You bring together all its aspects, integrating the parts in order to transform it by creating something new. You can manage your own internal differences and conflicts in the same way.

Often, when faced with two opposite interests, we seek to find a compromise in the middle. But this tends towards both sides giving something up; it tends towards mediocrity; it tends towards lose/lose. If one wins at the expense of the other, there will be an ongoing problem.

In Case notes 11 (page 91), Nick found himself in a dilemma. The part of him that wanted to succeed in a tough culture found itself in conflict with the part of him that

valued fairness and honesty. His behavior at work
developed so that he would be tough in front of his boss,
followed by compensatory behavior because he felt guilty.
Consequently, he felt compromised whatever he did and his
colleagues resented him for his rather transparent posturing.
He was also tough on himself, working punishing hours and
sacrificing other aspects of his life, like his relationship, and
then compensating by buying himself and his partner
expensive items and holidays, trying to make amends.
At this stage Nick was compromising: sometimes tough,
sometimes kind; sometimes punishing, sometimes
compensating. The result was that he felt he could not get
the balance right. The compromises did not work.

In order to transform this situation to one where Nick
stopped feeling compromised, a passive victim bouncing
between one extreme of behavior and the other, he
needed to examine what was acceptable to him and what
he really wanted to achieve. By doing this he could make
conscious choices and either accept or eliminate the
causes of his conflict.

Toughness ————————————————— Fairness
                    Compromised
                    behavior

Nick can now act more in line with his beliefs. Going
against what he feels is fair on his colleagues was the main
cause of his internal conflict. He is able to work within his

Accept or eliminate
causes of conflict

Toughness                    Fairness
                Compromised
                behavior

own sphere of influence to behave differently. One response, building a competent team to support him, eliminated one of the causes of the conflict between his personal life and his work. This enabled him to work more efficiently for fewer hours and, importantly, had the effect of improving the job satisfaction and the sense of value of the people in his team. Because they now feel more respected and valued by Nick, and because he sometimes openly chooses to be tough in order to improve performance, they are less resentful. He does not need to compensate for this toughness, because his reasons are genuine and transparent and in line with the values of the team, to do good work.

I remember negotiating a deal for a management buyout team to buy their company, XH, from its corporate owner, ZB. I wanted to get the cheapest deal for my client and ZB needed a certain price to avoid having to show a book loss in its accounts. In the negotiations we became totally polarized in our extreme positions. There were bad feeling, resentment and blame between the management and the owner, and we did not manage to move significantly away from these positions, so the deal was never made.

Book value ———————————————————— Cheapest price
Lose/lose

Had we thought about it, we might have looked more closely at the real needs of the situation. Both companies had originally been employee owned and were proud of the ethical stance they normally took to business. It was important to all concerned to preserve the jobs of the 60 people employed by ZB. Had the management of the two companies made that their purpose, instead of using the situation to vent their frustration with each other, they would have been united in finding a solution. Having made the purchase, which had no real commercial logic, XH soon became frustrated in its efforts to turn ZB around. This required more time and money than it had expected.

XH needed to be free of ZB so that it could focus its time on more important matters, but the chief executive at XH did not want to have to admit that he had made a mistake. Since relationships had become strained, the managers at ZB were enjoying seeing him suffer.

The best solution for ZB as a company would have been a sale to a larger competitor with a different geographic spread and strong marketing. ZB was worth more to an existing manufacturer than to a buyout team, which could have closed the gap in valuations. Both could have come out feeling they had done a good job, finding their rewards in practicing the values they held. The error came earlier, so it was unjustifiable to use this later situation to repair it. If the management of ZB had performed well in a more favorable environment, perhaps they would have found more exciting careers in a larger company. At least they would have avoided buying a company that would always struggle as a small operator.

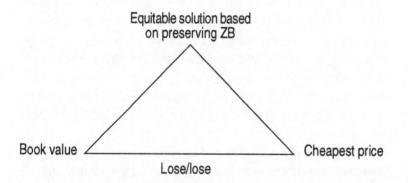

Transformation is not the same as compromise. It is seeing the situation in its proper context and having the satisfaction of finding the best solution.

In his book *The Prophet*, Kahlil Gibran looks at the polarities of reason and passion.[3] Reason alone lacks imagination and is confining. Passion alone lacks firm ground and, left unbounded, will burn itself out. A compromise would be to lose some of the powers of both reason and passion, or to sometimes act with reason and sometimes with passion. But Gibran's solution is different, fully using the qualities of each rather than making them mutually exclusive:

> Let your soul exalt your reason to the height of passion, that it may sing;
> And let it direct your passion with reason, that your passion may live through its own daily resurrection, and like the phoenix rise above its own ashes.

I have recently been working within AstraZeneca on the merger of part of those two companies. Astra was very decentralized, with its primary emphasis on individual creativity in science. Its five sites all had different cultures and operating procedures. Zeneca, based largely on one site, concentrated on being a global player, with a high degree of standardization of operating procedures. In the merger, the fears of people in Astra were centered on losing personal creativity and becoming bogged down in bureaucracy. The fears within Zeneca centered on lack of professional rigor and poor prioritization of projects. The polarization formed around standardization and creativity. If people merely fight their corner for the supremacy of their view in the new company, the likely result would be a hotchpotch of procedures neither owned nor adhered to by the employees of either the former Astra or the former Zeneca.

People within AstraZeneca have to enter a debate on what will serve the new company best in the long term, leaving aside their own self-interest, but within the context of their values and purpose in relation to work. They do not need a compromise between standardization and creativity.

Standardization ————————————————— Creativity
Degraded standards
and creativity

Standardization keeps costs down, cuts out duplication and enhances quality standards for both employees and customers. Creativity is the lifeblood of a pharmaceutical company, producing new chemical compounds and innovative product applications. Both of these are needed. Creativity is needed to ensure that standardization achieves its objectives. Standardization is needed to ensure that good ideas have sufficient resources backing them and the means to bring innovative, useful and safe products to global markets. This reflects the values and purpose of the company.

The transformation comes by reframing the problem in the context of the values and purpose. So, reflecting the words of Kahlil Gibran, let them exalt standardization to the height of creativity, that it may serve its purpose, and let them direct creativity with appropriate standardization, that creativity may live in the daily work and rise above its own chaos into form.

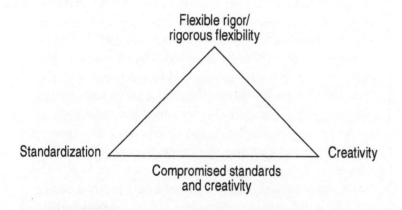

Flexible rigor/
rigorous flexibility

Standardization

Creativity

Compromised standards
and creativity

---

**CASE NOTES 19**
**TRANSFORMING A SITUATION**

A participant on an inner leadership course had a situation that she needed to resolve. Karen was the curator of a museum. Over 12 years, she had built specialist expertise relevant to the objects under her care. The governors of the museum decided to change the way in which it was managed, and issued Karen with a new job description without any consultation.

She could see that the changes would be detrimental to the preservation of some of the pieces, but was told that no discussion would be allowed. She was instructed to fulfill the new contract or quit. She felt resentful, sad and powerless. She could only see two responses:

Fulfill new contract ——————————————————— Quit

Lose/lose

Karen's feelings kept her from seeing the situation differently. If she were to quit, the resentful part of her would be saying: 'That would show them. They would soon know how much they needed me.' The sad part did not want to quit, for the sake of the collection and because she had put so much of her life into the job. The powerless part thought that there was no option but to fulfill the new contract and do her best, because she could not afford to lose her job.

Karen could now see these parts clearly, and therefore stand back from them. Resentment was useful to the extent that it gave her energy, the energy of anger, but it clouded her judgment. The sad part put her in touch with her values. She really did care about the collection and she knew she had done her job well in the past. Feeling powerless made her aware that she was not powerless. She used the parts of each of these that were useful to her to reframe the situation.

Karen's purpose was one of stewardship, preserving important works of art, for their value to history, aesthetics and culture. She decided that she could find work elsewhere if her current position became untenable. If she quit, she would use that to bring attention to the situation. Her choice was to write her own job description, setting out the terms under which she would be prepared to continue her employment, explaining in detail her reasons.

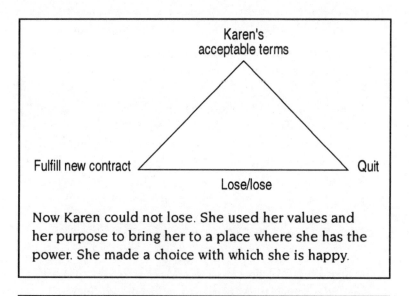

Now Karen could not lose. She used her values and her purpose to bring her to a place where she has the power. She made a choice with which she is happy.

## Exercise 27 – Transforming conflict

Think of some situations in your current work life that are causing you conflict, both with others and within yourself. See if you can think of five or six.

Put each side of the conflict at the two ends of the bottom line of a triangle. Using what you have learned from the examples above, write between them the effect of making a compromise between the two.

Now think of how each separate situation relates to your values and purpose. Bearing those in mind, what would transform the conflict and allow both ends of the polarity to be used?

In the next exercise, you can use your will to turn this increased awareness into a plan of action and practical steps.

## Exercise 28 – Self-leading

As you do this exercise, be as self-aware as you can. Observe your physical reactions, your emotions and your thoughts. See which mindsets and constituents are around you. Remember that you have a deep, still place, the center of your awareness and will, to guide you.

1   **Purpose and intention.** Consider one of the situations you want to transform. Think about its importance to you. How does it fit with your values and purpose? What is your vision here? When you think of it, do you feel excitement and passion? State your overall intention. Why is it so important to you to achieve this transformation? And why now? Answering these will show you if you are likely to have sufficient motivation to carry it through.

2   **Deliberation.** Take time over this. Make an assessment of where the achievement of transforming this conflict will take you. Where do you feel you are now in relation to it? What constituents and mindsets are active that may be influencing the way you see things and broadening or narrowing your choices? Define how large the gap is between your current state or situation and how things would be if the situation is transformed. Saturate yourself with both internal and external information. Let ideas come without judging them. Generate as many options as you can, at least three and preferably more. Your will may bring in things that have not been readily available to your conscious mind. List as many ways as you can in which you could move towards what you want. Remember, this is about taking achievable steps towards it. Suspend your judgment, gather information.

3   **Choice.** Ask yourself some very exact questions that you need to answer in order to refine your options, such as what might be the consequences of an option, how far it would take you, what would make it possible for you. Make a transformation triangle for each, showing the two sides of the situation, a compromise between them and a transformation at the apex. This will highlight the differences between the options you have available. Use the transformation triangles to move away from compromise to

finding new ways of seeing the differences between the choices. Now *make* a choice, a choice to take one or more significant steps. Listen for internal hints that may guide you. Be aware of things you notice and things that happen to you. Then make that choice. Check your choice by observing your physical reactions, your emotions and your initial thoughts.

4  **Affirmation.** Affirm your choice by writing down what you have decided to do, and put a date by which you will have achieved that. Make any preliminary arrangements that you need to make to start the process off. You could tell someone else about it in order to strengthen your resolve.

5  **Planning.** Work up a plan to implement your choice, keeping in mind your purpose and the underlying values. Add in the details, setting tasks and dates. How will you gather any resources you need to start?

6  **Implementation.** Once you have a workable plan, you can move on to implementation. You should find that the importance to you of what you are doing and the alignment between that and your values give you the motivation you need to implement your plan. The careful consideration you have given your choice of action, with all the options you have been through, has increased the creativity with which you have approached it. The planning you have carried out will increase your confidence in being able to implement the plan. As a result, you may find the implementation much less effort than you imagined.

---

You can repeat the above exercise to review the main purpose of your life. I recommend that you do this.

# 15 *The Benefits of Inner Leadership*

You are now practicing inner leadership. You are focused on your purpose and your values, which can now act as a framework to shape your decisions, your actions and your behavior. You are more often able to choose from which part of yourself you want to act. You have a systematic process for realizing your self-leading potential and for meeting the real needs of each situation creatively. You are on solid ground. You can live from the essence of your being.

You will not always do this correctly. You may forget. You may see the situation and respond in the old way. You may be self-critical sometimes. Don't worry and don't judge yourself. Remember: 'Perfection is unattainable, but that is no reason to despair.' Make that your mantra. You owe it to yourself. Enjoy the higher self-esteem that comes from being able to actualize your purpose and act according to your values. Give yourself scope for innovation, invention and improvement.

## REALIZING YOUR SELF-LEADING POTENTIAL

You are becoming more of who you are by *remembering* who you are. There has been no attempt in this book to ask you to be someone you are not already. You may have started *Inner Leadership* because you wanted to be a more effective leader within your own sphere of influence. Just by getting to this stage, and by practicing what you have learned about yourself, you already are.

Your inner world influences your outer world. The outer world affects your inner world, causing you to redefine yourself according to each new reality. Through our interactions with people and in situations we experience ourselves more fully. This is 'life's rich pageant'. We can also attract the experiences that will help us to fulfill our purpose. People who are focused on their purpose usually fulfill it. In this way we influence our own futures.

An organization is the sum of all the energy that has ever passed through it. An organization is very similar to us as individuals, like a building in which many people dwell. In the same way that some of our constituents exert a greater influence over us, some of the individuals who pass through organizations exert a greater influence.

**FROM THE INDIVIDUAL TO THE ORGANIZATION**

We can influence existing organizations. Practicing inner leadership has the effect of turning up your energy voltage, increasing your influence considerably.

It is important to remember that you are dealing with culture, history, deeply held beliefs, patterns and constituents that have been forming since your organization began, just like the ones you find in yourself. In addition, all the individuals have personal histories.

To take the lead, your main resource lies in your ability to lead yourself and apply those principles in your dealings with others and when facing situations.

## GAINING THE BENEFITS OF INNER LEADERSHIP

I don't know your circumstances, so I can't tell you exactly how you should apply inner leadership. But I know you can now apply it and create your vision of yourself as a leader, whether that is as a chief executive, or a creative artist, or an innovative scientist, or an exceptional manager of people, or a computer whizz, or a strategic thinker, or an intuitive person, or someone with a deep understanding of people and culture, or however you see yourself.

As I have said before, inner leadership gives you the clarity to respond to the real needs of a new situation with awareness, aptitude and purpose. I stand by that as the most important outcome of your work. Below, I briefly cover this and other areas where being a self-leader practicing inner leadership can bring you significant benefit.

**Respond to the real needs of each situation**. By increasing your awareness of yourself and your relationship with the outside world, you align your interests and the needs of the situation facing you. Not to serve the situation is not to serve yourself. By knowing your ground and being able to choose your response from a wide range of options, by acting out of your essence, you can now stand back from situations and assess them without being drawn into a quick reaction. You can give yourself time to see which constituents and mindsets come rushing in first. You will know when you are being drawn into serving one of your old defense mechanisms, or making the fear choice, which may provide short-term comfort but will serve neither you nor the situation in the longer term.

CHOOSING THE RIGHT RESPONSE

*Create win/win situations*

Remember the case of Jack Evans, the finance director who abstained on the issue of the acquisition (Case notes 12, page 104). Jack abstained because he felt this would serve his own position best. He abstained out of fear of confrontation with his CEO and fear of not providing himself with enough salary and pension for his future. He was serving his own defense mechanisms, and at one level who can blame him? But he got himself into a lose/lose situation. He lost the respect of his CEO, the confidence of his board of directors and his job. The company later faced bankruptcy, at great cost to its shareholders and its employees. If Jack had responded to the situation's needs, he would have voted against the acquisition. He would have had to withstand some short-term discomfort, but he would have retained the respect of his peers and, more importantly, his self-respect. He would have been in a win/win situation.

By applying values and setting behaviors according to those values, behaviors that can be monitored and checked, you are giving yourself and your team members a framework in which to work and make decisions. Each time you face a new situation, your values and purpose will guide you to make an appropriate decision.

**Act with integrity and congruence**. You now have a strong sense of who you are. You have a considerable amount of self-knowledge. You have identified values and a purpose, which are your solid ground. You are able to accept parts of yourself that hitherto you preferred not to know about and that unconsciously influenced you. From this position, it is very difficult not to act with integrity and congruence. You will certainly know when you are not, and from there you can choose. Andrew, in Case notes 1 on GCV, knew exactly when he was acting with integrity and when he was not.

**Improve relationships and increase autonomy**. Because you now stand on such solid ground in relation to yourself, other people's views will no longer be a threat to your ego or the vulnerable parts of yourself. This will give you a more accurate understanding of what is happening. You know you don't have to agree with other people, so you can listen and still say no, while on the other hand you can also change your mind. This open and non-threatening attitude brings a spirit of cooperation without needing to compromise, without losing your autonomy.

*Gain cooperation and remain autonomous*

Exercise 26 in Chapter 12, about listening before speaking, is well worth practicing. Many people have never experienced what it is like to be listened to, intently and without judgment. Even those who feel they have good relationships often comment on how wonderful it feels to be listened to at such a level. It is an intimate experience. Not only will you understand your colleagues better, but also they will feel respected and valued.

**Inspire loyalty, trust and confidence**. If you are acting with integrity and congruence, people will know more about who you are, which includes the more difficult parts of yourself. You don't always have to be nice, but equally you don't have an axe to grind, so you don't need to score points off other people. This is particularly valuable when dealing with people in more senior positions, who may feel threatened by your higher level of participation.

*Inspire love*

You will earn the trust of people by being who you are, by being real. You will be able to be challenging and confronting when necessary, without the threat that conflict could end in punishment or long-term animosity. You are genuinely interested in the views of other people. They will see you as someone whose actions are value based, whose intentions are good. Through acting like this you will become someone to emulate. You will inspire loyalty, trust and confidence, and even love. Where there is deep trust, others can come to see you in the same light. People will want to work with you and give you their best.

When people with this quality collaborate, they can transform the way they work together, overcoming many of the difficulties they previously encountered. There is a multiplier effect at work on their level of confidence.

*Generating trust*

### CASE NOTES 20 – A TEAM OF SELF-LEADERS

I have been working with a team of six managers, in charge of a business with a £200 million turnover. The underlying culture of the company is one of mistrust, secrets and power. Through our work the managers have realized that trust is the greatest issue they face if they are to improve their performance. They see this as trust of each other, but first and foremost it is trust of themselves. They work in a culture that encourages mistakes to be covered up. They are all afraid of being scapegoats and blamed for things that go wrong. Consequently, they are unable to be open with one another. They don't share information if it reflects badly on them, so problems are seen late, with detrimental results.

Our work has been to change this, by bringing these matters to their attention. I work separately with each person, to support them in taking the courage to be more open and honest with both themselves and others. They are learning to understand and trust each other, they are feeling better about themselves and they are being more open with clients. One said:

> I can now meet clients with more confidence, sure that I am not going to put my foot in it because one of my colleagues has told them something I didn't know about. With truth on the table, we can work more closely with our clients to provide them with a better service.

This is having a positive effect on the individuals, but also on the way they behave together as a team. They can talk about things openly, support each other and learn from each other. There is less suspicion and cynicism. They have learned to make direct and truthful statements that are based on their own experience and non-threatening to others. It affects their relationships with the employees in their departments and has a beneficial effect on the company. They are beginning to experience the multiplier effect.

**Be able to change by adapting your self-concept**. You know now that your self-concept is much more flexible than it has been before. You can choose to identify or not with parts of yourself, or to act from your center of identity. Words like 'can't' will fall from your vocabulary. An inflexible self-concept is a significant barrier to change. If you can be flexible yourself and not be afraid of change, you will be able to help other people to make changes too. As continuous change is now an accepted reality in

*Let go of your ego*

most organizations, your ability to be adaptable and able to change will be invaluable.

**Develop a strong sense of purpose**. By working through the processes of recognizing and exploring, you have been able to discover your purpose as a person and as a leader. That sense of purpose is invaluable for guiding yourself and others. Use this as a context for every decision you make. Compare how your purpose fits with that of the organization. Does something need to happen to align these?

**Discover and apply your values**. It is important to use values in leadership. To quote Robert de Haas again, chief executive of Levi Strauss: 'Values provide a common language for aligning a company's leadership and its people.' Values can be used to give people greater guidance on what is expected from them in terms of their attitudes and behavior. In a changing environment, they can provide an element of stability and predictability. This gives people greater autonomy and allows leaders to delegate more confidently. This is the basis of true empowerment, where people have the tools and the autonomy to make more of their own decisions. This is really strengthened if people agree with the values, and even more so if they helped to form them.

*Accept contradictions*

**Work with paradox and conflict**. Because you are so sure of your ground, you are now able to work with what you found difficult and threatening in the past. You now know you are full of different parts representing opposite ends of the spectrum, and you are able to accept both. Working with paradox becomes natural; it makes more sense than it used to. Conflict becomes less threatening to you and to others, because you are able to stand back from it now, to observe what is happening outside in the same way as you have been able to observe what is happening inside you. This does not mean that you won't sometimes be angry, hurt or disappointed, because these may be valid responses to situations. But you are much more likely to be able to come back from this position and discuss what is happening openly with others. This will engender an atmosphere of openness and trust, in which all the members of your team can fully participate and contribute their full creativity.

**Empathize with others and know how to motivate them**. Your increased psychological knowledge of yourself will give you a greater ability to understand other people's worlds. Empathy is being able to put yourself in somebody else's shoes for a while. Receiving genuine empathy is a remarkable experience. To have someone's full attention, and to have them reflecting back to you what you are saying so that you know they have understood your position as far as possible, creates a situation of intimacy, respect and understanding. By understanding the deeper worlds of other people, you will be able to respond to their needs more fully, which will motivate them. You can do this because you know you will be able to respond to people in a genuine way without being compromised or pulled off course by them emotionally.

By practicing the self-awareness exercise, you will be able to monitor your physical, emotional and thinking responses, and so you will know if you are being manipulated. In fact, when you act with integrity and empathy, people are less likely to manipulate you. Their need to is not so great.

**Express your creativity and enhance problem solving**. You are now aware of the many facets of yourself, and you have the power to move between them. You should also now be able to extend the gap between seeing a problem and needing to solve it, meaning that a range of options can be considered. So many poor decisions are made in organisations because of pressure to come up with a solution to a problem as soon as possible.

Try delaying by at least one sleep cycle answering a problem that you would normally attempt to solve

*Unleash your creativity*

immediately. Allow the problem to exist in the back of your mind. Play with it. You will be surprised at the number of insights you get for doing things in new and creative ways. The 'insight in the bath' syndrome really works, because it allows in your unconscious mind, which is much more resourceful than your conscious mind.

*Not to be confused with bravado*

**Increase your self-confidence**. We have to be careful about this, because sometimes apparently high self-confidence is covering a sense of insecurity. If we are talking realistically, I would be very surprised if your self-confidence is not at a much higher level than it was when you started this book. If you are self-confident, then people will place more confidence in you and grow in confidence themselves. When you act with genuine self-confidence you can stand back from a situation, allow others to put their ideas first and let them take the credit, which will bring out the best in them.

**Learn how to mentor others to greater inner leadership**. Now that you have been through the process, you are in a position to help others gain a greater degree of inner leadership. You could suggest that they use this book and offer to act as their mentor. But remember to have respect for them and never push somebody into this or further than they are happy to go. One of the things that I know will have kept you working at a safe level throughout this book is your natural ability to gauge the depth at which you can work at any time. Allow others to do that as well.

**BEWARE OF SELF-INFLATION**

This is very important. Watch out for feelings of self-importance now that you have worked through this book. It is possible to create another constituent, which you may call the 'fully realized being', but which is merely inflated ego.

Watch out for signs such as:

- talking about the experiences this book has brought you at every opportunity until people are fed up with hearing about it;
- immediately trying to get everyone to use it;
- loss of sense of humor in relation to this work;
- defensiveness if people don't agree with your views;
- doing psychological profiles on everyone;
- thinking you are now God's gift to leadership;
- comparing yourself favorably with everyone else;
- feeling generally superior;
- suddenly giving up people or activities that used to be important to you because they are no longer 'good enough';
- undergoing a large change in the way you speak or the language you use.

Check out with a friend, a spouse, a colleague, your mentor or co-mentor that you are not falling into this trap. There are real dangers that this could happen to you. These are signs that you are not acting from a balanced and central position.

Please, be humble about this work. It is very powerful and it makes you very powerful. It is so important to remain in contact with your purpose and your values so that you don't abuse that power. There will be times when you press buttons in other people and they react strongly to you. Don't retaliate.

The work you have started here is an ongoing process. You will never fully complete it. There will always be more. What you have gained at any stage of your life will be extremely useful to you, but it is not the whole picture. After a while, doing this work becomes a way of life. In my experience, if it is treated lightly, it is challenging, stimulating and enjoyable. There are also times when it is extremely hard and causes anxiety. When I trained in psychosynthesis, a common comment from those graduating was: 'Had I known beforehand how hard it would be at times, I would never have started. Now that I have finished, I wouldn't have missed it for anything!'

*This is an ongoing process*

## CONGRATULATIONS

You have come a long way through this book if you have reached this point and done many of the exercises. It will have taken you a considerable time, but more than that, you will have pushed yourself to the limits of your being.

I want to say how much I appreciate you for doing this, and I want you to appreciate yourself for it. Congratulations. Give yourself a very large pat on the back. Give yourself a treat. Perhaps you could buy yourself a present to remind you of what you have achieved.

In 1991 I had a major breakthrough in my life. Following this I bought myself an expensive pen, which I often used. It reminded me of what I had done and to appreciate myself. I lost the pen on the day that completed the episode of my life begun by the original breakthrough. But that's another story.

*Contact me at*
*www.inner-leadership.com*

I would love you to write to me with your experiences to add to my research, and it would give me pleasure to hear of your achievements and personally appreciate you. My website is www.inner-leadership.com. Please use it. You can also use the site to communicate with other people practicing inner leadership, receive a newsletter and keep up to date with events through the inner leadership network.

*And finally*

Keep using inner leadership, going deeper. See this as a process of continuous change. Good luck!

# Psychosynthesis

*Inner Leadership* is based on an applied psychology that is widely used around the world in a broad range of applications and in a number of different areas of life. There follows a brief description of the history, purpose and process for those readers who wish to know more about it.

## HISTORY

Psychosynthesis was developed by Roberto Assagioli between 1910 and his death in 1974. He developed it theoretically, applied it practically and expounded it in more than 300 papers and two books, *The Act of Will*[1] and *Psychosynthesis: a Manual of Principles and Techniques*[2]. Numerous other books and hundreds of articles have been written and there are psychosynthesis centres and institutes in 10 countries.

Born in Italy in 1888, Assagioli formed his views at a very exciting time in central Europe. He was a young medical doctor, specializing in neurology, when Einstein was developing the theory of relativity in Berne, Freud was developing psychoanalysis in Vienna, Jung was developing analytical psychology in Zurich, Lenin was forming the Russian Revolution in Zurich, Heidegger was preparing to launch his existential theories in Freiburg and James Joyce was writing *Ulysses* in Trieste.

## THE PURPOSE OF PSYCHOSYNTHESIS

Assagioli proposed that the purpose of psychosynthesis was to contact a deeper sense of identity and to use this to integrate the various aspects of the personality into a synthesized whole. This is achieved by gaining greater self-awareness and applying to this your will, your power to act autonomously. His hypothesis set out that what we encounter in life – the problems and the obstacles, the triumphs and the joys – is inherently meaningful, coherent and potentially transformative. He maintained, as later did Maslow, that there is a pull towards meaning, purpose and integration, which Assagioli called self-realization and Maslow self-actualization.

The main premise of psychosynthesis is simple: psychological factors, of which we are often unaware or unconscious, greatly influence our thinking and our behavior. By increasing our awareness of our attitudes and behaviors, of the deep beliefs and mindsets we hold, of the various constituents of our personalities, of our purpose and values and of our hopes and fears, we can free ourselves to choose how we approach situations and problems and how we behave, and to achieve what we want in life – our purpose.

Each one of us has values that we hold as important and a purpose that is uniquely ours. These deeply held values and purpose lead us to live in service of something greater than ourselves, a guiding principle. We may serve the company for which we work, but also through that we serve a greater community, perhaps as great as humanity itself. For example, people working in a pharmaceutical company at one level serve their own needs for employment and remuneration, for belonging to a company and to a scientific community, but they may also feel that they serve the principle of alleviating human suffering and pain or extending the frontiers of human knowledge. We may serve our families, but also through that serve a philosophical ideal of a greater family, of care, of responsibility, of parenthood.

By coming to know ourselves 'inside out' we understand ourselves. We discover a part of ourselves capable of standing back and observing our inner processes, giving an inner clarity, our 'center of identity'. The discovery of our will, a deep energy, enables us to choose what we want, to make decisions based on reality and to work for our own good. By understanding ourselves more deeply, we come to accept ourselves as we are at the same time as being able to explore our potentiality.

So the purpose of psychosynthesis is to enhance the quality and effectiveness of our lives by increasing our levels of choice within a broader context of meaning. Psychosynthesis lays down a disciplined process for self-discovery and personal development. Using our inherent will to develop and grow as people, we can align our behaviors and actions with our purpose and values. By increasing our self-awareness and galvanizing our inner power to be autonomous and to act in alignment with our values and purpose, we create our lives in such a way as to fulfill our purpose. It is a way of looking at our mental, emotional and spiritual world, the psyche.

## BRIDGING WHAT IS AND WHAT IS WANTED

Psychosynthesis and inner leadership encourage us to examine our lives to see 'what is' and also to see how we want to be, giving us a bifocal vision. We can then find ways of bridging the gap. Using our values and our purpose, reinforced with the energy of our will to direct and organize our inner resources, we are enabled to live more meaningful, creative and fulfilling lives for the good of ourselves and for others.

## THE PROCESS OF PSYCHOSYNTHESIS

Each person is an individual, and the psychosynthesis of each takes its own unique path. In this book I have set out a method with exercises, which is particularly suited to people working in organizations.

Within the overall process we can identify two stages. In the first stage the integration of the personality takes place around the center of identity, and the individual attains a healthy level of functioning in terms of their work and relationships. Much of *Inner Leadership* is within that part of the process.

In the second stage, the person moves towards alignment with their guiding principle, their overall purpose and values, expressing qualities such as compassion, global responsibility, cooperation and love for others. It is here that *Inner Leadership* takes up the challenge of how do we want to be in our organizational roles and what sorts of organizations we want to work in. These two stages often overlap.

The general program of psychosynthesis normally contains the following elements:

- A realistic assessment of the psyche and the personality, recognizing unconscious aspects.
- Exploring who we truly are, by exploring our identifications, implying a degree of awakening to the realization of our centre of identity as distinct from the psychic contents with which we habitually identify.
- The bringing together of the parts of ourselves around the center of identity to form an integrated, autonomous being. This calls for the use of the will and the imagination and the strengthening of all underdeveloped qualities.
- The application of these in our chosen field.

This general program is put into practice by means of the systematic use of a number of techniques.

# References

**Preface**
1   *Out of the Crisis*, W Edwards Deming, Cambridge University
    Press, 1986.

**Chapter 1  Inner Leadership**
1   'The work of leadership', RA Heifetz and DL Laurie, *Harvard
    Business Review*, Jan/Feb 1997.
2   *The Dance of Change*, Peter Senge *et al.*, Nicholas Brealey
    Publishing, 1999.

**Chapter 2  Recognizing Yourself**
1   *Emotional Intelligence*, Daniel Goleman, Bloomsbury, 1996.

**Stage 2  Exploring**
1   *Leadership is an Art*, Max De Pree, Dell Books, 1990.
2   *Smart Choices: a Practical Guide to Making Better Decisions*, JS
    Hammond, RL Keeney and H Raiffa, Harvard Business
    School Press, 1998.

**Chapter 4  How We Become Who We Are**
1   *The Dance of Change*.

2   *The Reengineering Revolution Handbook*, Michael Hammer and Steven Stanton, HarperBusiness, 1995.

### Chapter 5  Exploring your Constituents
1   *The Act of Will: a Guide to Self-actualization and Self-realization*, Roberto Assagioli, Crucible, 1990.
2   *What We May Be: the Visions and Techniques of Psychosynthesis*, Piero Ferruci, Mandala, 1990.
3   *Farther Reaches of Human Nature*, Abraham Maslow, Penguin Arkana, 1993.

### Chapter 6  Exploring your Mindsets
1   *Global Mind Change: the Promise of the Twenty-first Century*, Willis Harman, Berrett-Koehler & Institute of Noetic Sciences, 2nd edn 1998.
2   NUTS! *SouthWest Airlines' Crazy Recipe for Business and Personal Success*, Kevin Freiberg and Jackie Freiberg, Bard Press, 1996.
3   *The Living Company*, Arie de Geus, Nicholas Brealey Publishing, 1997.

### Chapter 7  Discovering Your Values
1   *Farther Reaches of Human Nature*.
2   NUTS!
3   *Farther Reaches of Human Nature*.

### Chapter 8  Knowing Your Purpose
1   Institute of Psychosynthesis course materials.

### Chapter 9  How We Change
1   *Farther Reaches of Human Nature*.
2   *Neurosis and Treatment*, Andras Angyal, Wiley, 1965.
3   *Repression of the Sublime*, Frank Haronian, Psychosynthesis Research Foundation, 1971.
4   'The work of leadership'.

### Chapter 10  Your Center of Identity
1   *Learning to Lead*, Warren Bennis and Joan Goldsmith, Nicholas Brealey Publishing, 1997.

2  *Tao Te Ching*, Lao Tzu, Richard Wilhelm edition, Arkana, 1985.
3  *The Four Quartets*, TS Eliot, Faber and Faber, 1944.
4  *Myths to Live By*, Joseph Campbell, Viking, 1972.
5  *Farther Reaches of Human Nature.*

**Chapter 11  Freeing Yourself from Identification**
1  *Myths to Live by.*

**Chapter 12  Your Will**
1  *The Act of Will.*
2  *The Act of Will.*

**Chapter 13  Self-Acceptance**
1  *Tao Te Ching.*
2  *Farther Reaches of Human Nature.*

**Chapter 14  Self-Leading**
1  *The Prophet*, Kahlil Gibran, Wordsworth, 1996.

**Psychosynthesis**
1  *The Act of Will.*
2  *Psychosynthesis: a Manual of Principles and Techniques*, Roberto Assagioli, Mandala, 1990.

# *Index*

## ABOUT THE AUTHOR

Inner-Leadership.com Limited provides courses, consultancy services and mentoring in inner leadership. There is also a network for people practicing inner leadership.

If you want more information, please contact Simon Smith and David England:

on our website:

www.inner-leadership.com

by e-mail:

simon@inner-leadership.com
david@inner-leadership.com

by telephone:

+44 (0)1803 865154

by fax:

+44 (0)1803 840361

by post:

The Old Stables
Station Road
Totnes
Devon TQ9 5HW
UK